TURNING
MODIFIED
SLIMLINE
PENS

DON WARD

Beyond the basics

Schiffer Publishing Ltd

4880 Lower Valley Road • Atglen, PA 19310

D1597760

Other Schiffer Books on Related Subjects:
Dick Sing ReTurns: Unique and Unusual Pens from the Wood Lathe.
   Dick Sing. ISBN: 9780764303593. $14.99
Turning Pens and Desk Accessories. Mike Cripps. ISBN: 0764300512. $12.95

Copyright © 2012 by Don Ward

Library of Congress Control Number: 2012941915

All rights reserved. No part of this work may be reproduced or used in any form or by any means—graphic, electronic, or mechanical, including photocopying or information storage and retrieval systems—without written permission from the publisher.
The scanning, uploading and distribution of this book or any part thereof via the Internet or via any other means without the permission of the publisher is illegal and punishable by law. Please purchase only authorized editions and do not participate in or encourage the electronic piracy of copyrighted materials.
"Schiffer," "Schiffer Publishing, Ltd. & Design," and the "Design of pen and inkwell" are registered trademarks of Schiffer Publishing, Ltd.

Designed by Justin Watkinson
Cover by Bruce Waters
Type set in Bernhard Modern BT/Zurich BT

ISBN: 978-0-7643-4169-4
Printed in China

Schiffer Books are available at special discounts for bulk purchases for sales promotions or premiums. Special editions, including personalized covers, corporate imprints, and excerpts can be created in large quantities for special needs. For more information contact the publisher:

Published by Schiffer Publishing, Ltd.
4880 Lower Valley Road
Atglen, PA 19310
Phone: (610) 593-1777; Fax: (610) 593-2002
E-mail: Info@schifferbooks.com

For the largest selection of fine reference books on this and related subjects, please visit our website at **www.schifferbooks.com**
We are always looking for people to write books on new and related subjects.
If you have an idea for a book, please contact us at proposals@schifferbooks.com

This book may be purchased from the publisher.
Please try your bookstore first.
You may write for a free catalog.

In Europe, Schiffer books are distributed by
Bushwood Books
6 Marksbury Ave.
Kew Gardens
Surrey TW9 4JF England
Phone: 44 (0) 20 8392 8585; Fax: 44 (0) 20 8392 9876
E-mail: info@bushwoodbooks.co.uk
Website: www.bushwoodbooks.co.uk

DEDICATION

This book is dedicated to my wife who also happens to be my foremost fan. She lovingly offers her encouragement, her artistic talents, and her eye for design to my pen making. Thanks Ruth for all of your help and encouragement. I love you.

ACKNOWLEDGMENTS

I would like to take this opportunity to thank Dick and Cindy Sing for their initial encouragement to write this book and also for their continued support during the process. Thanks to Dick Sing for directing me to Schiffer Publishing, Ltd. Thanks also for the hard work of Jeff Snyder, my editor at Schiffer Publishing, Ltd.

Thanks also to Barry Gross for furnishing some of the materials I used to make the pens for this book. Barry furnished the acrylics sanding kit, some of the pen kits used for the book's pens, the maple burl blanks, and the pen case used to hold pens for some of the book's pictures. Barry's website is www.bgartforms.com

CONTENTS

(1) Plug end with Base wax (dental) or play dough P

(2) use skew from center to both ends to avoid tear out P

(3) 5 minute epoxy for a couple of kits 3 P13
30 minute epoxy for several kits 3 P13

(4) White out Correction fluid to write on blank P 19

(5) length from end of transmission is always 3.95" P 19

FOREWORD

The making of turned wooden pens has been around for many years. Over the years, the pen craze has blossomed into a growing hobby and market to many. There were only a few commercial pen kits available, with the quality leaving a lot to be desired in fit and finish. Today there are a multitude of different styles, ranging from pencils, ballpoint, roller ball, and fountain pens. The quality has grown greatly both in the manufacture of parts, and in the quality and types of finishes.

The majority of pen turners selects one of the pen kits available on the market, and fits it with the wood of their desire. To most, the species, color, grain pattern, or some other feature of the wood used is the normal path taken. There is a select faction of pen turners who are never satisfied with the ordinary. These turners are the reason for the use of stabilized blanks, acrylics, laminated blanks, snakeskin wrapped pens, or materials that boggle the mind.

Don Ward is one of these turners. He has created processes and utilizes materials that have advanced the art of pen turning. Don is a competent demonstrator and has authored many articles to help with the teaching of pen turning.

With Don's innovations, he has helped raise the bar on the advancement of pens.

—Dick Sing

INTRODUCTION

Purpose of This Book

The main purpose of this book is to show several ways to modify or customize the Slimline pen kit. This book is not intended to teach beginning pen turning, but to show that the techniques used to make unique "slimline" pens are not beyond a beginning pen turner. The author assumes the readers of this book already know how to turn pens and are familiar with the Slimline kit. Although this book is not a beginning pen turning book, the first project will be a Slimline pen made according to the kit instructions. Then, several unique modifications will follow.

The Slimline Pen Kit

The Slimline pen kit is often the starter kit for new pen turners. The reasons why vary but here are some reasons that seem to be the most popular:

- The kits are cheaper than other kits. Often purchased in quantity the kits can cost under $2.00 each.
- Sales persons at woodturning stores often suggest that beginners start with the Slimline.
- Beginning pen turning classes at woodworking stores use the Slimline kit for their beginning pen turning classes.
- The Slimline may be the first kit new pen turners see.
- The Slimline is easy to make.

All of these reasons are true, except maybe the last one. Turning a pen with a straight barrel from one end to the other is not a beginner skill. New pen turners may not be new woodturners, but often they are. Also, turning a Slimline to the intended diameter means the finished pen barrel will have a veneer of wood somewhere in the .075" thickness. One small catch can rip the wood right off the brass tube. I do not consider the Slimline to be an easy pen to make or the best pen for the beginning pen turner. Pens that have a thicker layer of wood over the tube may be a better choice for beginners.

The Slimline was one of the very first kits available to woodturners who started making pens on the wood lathe. Other kits have come and gone, but the "lowly" Slimline has passed the test of time and is still one of the most popular kits available for making pens. There are several styles of Slimline kits. They are mostly the same with center band, clip, and diameter differences.

"Lowly" is used to describe the Slimline in a very honorable way. Many consider the Slimline kit to be the bottom of the heap of pen kits. Nothing could be further from the truth! How could it have stayed with us for thirty years if that was the case? I consider the Slimline to be the King of Pen Kits. It is the most forgiving of all the kits. Barrel lengths are not critical, within reason, as they are with other kits, such as the kits that use the Parker® style refill. Upper and lower barrels can be made longer or shorter than designed. The center band can be tossed and the barrels can be made with diameters larger than normal. For those of us who like to investigate design ideas, play with pen kits, see what we can create, and push designs to the limit, the Slimline is the kit to use.

The price of Slimline kits lend themselves to be the perfect pen to use for experimenting, playing, or giving as gifts. Kits are available in 10K and 22K gold plating, gold and black titanium, bright chrome, satin chrome, gun metal, satin gold, satin nickel, satin pearl, rhodium, platinum, and several anodized platings of various colors. Some platings wear and last better than others, Of course, the 10K and 22K gold are the least durable. Chrome is an excellent choice and on the lower end price-wise. Of course platinum, titanium, and rhodium are the most desirable platings because of their excellent durability but are also the

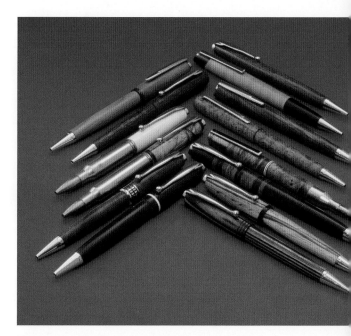

This photo shows some of the author's pens made using slimline kit parts.

most expensive. Purchased in quantities for volume discounts, the Slimline kits range from under $2.00 per kit upwards to $8.00 or more depending on where the kits are purchased.

Most vendors offer some kind of discount that is keyed to the number of kits purchased. Purchase more kits and the price per kit is lowered. The price breaks usually kick in at 10, 20, 30, etc. kits. One price is charged for fewer than 10 kits. Then, the price drops for 10-19 kits. Another price drop for 20-29 kits and so on. Some vendors allow for mixing platings within the same kit family and others do not. Check individual vendors for discount policies.

Tool Selection

One should use the tool or tools that have been mastered and feel comfortable. That being said, the rough out gouge is the normal tool for roughing out a pen blank. The next tool to be used is a spindle gouge for shaping the pen blank into a pen barrel. The next tool to use might be a skew or scraper to put the final cut onto the pen. While this progression is fine, some pen turners use the rough out gouge totally while others use the spindle gouge exclusively. And, the skew is also used by others from start to finish. The skew offers the best surface but is a difficult tool for many to master. In the last two years or so, carbide tipped tools have gained wide acceptance in the pen turning world. Carbide tips are secured to the tool bar with a small screw and when the cutter becomes dull the tip is rotated to a new cutting surface. There are several choices of carbide tipped tools. All of these tools are used on the pens made for this book. But, the author must admit the skew chisel is his tool of choice and the one he uses ninety-five percent of the time.

Pen Blank Materials

Wooden pen blanks are still very popular for making pens. Wooden pen blanks come as natural wood and burls along with resin impregnated or stabilized wood blanks. Other materials include many kinds of acrylic, polyester resin, urethane resin, and other similar materials. Powdered stone is mixed with acrylic resin to make Truestone® blanks. The list of acrylic and resin blanks is way too long to mention all of them here. Check with your favorite supplier for manmade materials.

Other materials include antler, horn, snakeskin encapsulated in clear resin, feathers encapsulated in clear resin, along with other natural materials used in their natural state or encapsulated or mixed with resin. The selection of pen blank materials is so much larger and diverse than it was just a few years ago and new blanks are being created on a regular basis.

Pen blank kits are available that use laser cut pieces as inlay and they are called laser inlay blanks. Many themes are covered using laser cut inlay kits, including flags of both nations and states, musical instruments, tools, animals, various geometric designs, religious icons, and others. Those who make these inlay kits also do custom work designed by the pen maker. Check out the laser inlay kits at www.kallenshaanwoods.com.

Pen Kits

Pen kits come in many sizes from skinny to fat, long to short, big to smaller, ballpoint, rollerball, and fountain pen. A pen kit is available for most any taste in style, size, and type. Motif and designs range from simple and conservative to complex and not so conservative, from plain to art nouveau, and even kits with lots of bling. Double and single barrel kits are common. Both click and twist ball points are also common.

Finishes

What is the best finish to use for my pens? This seems to be one of the most asked questions of those who make pens. Much has been written about finishes and how to use and apply them. Each finish has its set of pros and cons. I will not attempt to discuss finishes since so much other material is available. My friend and fellow pen turner, the late Russ Fairfield, has written extensively about finishes, both for pens and other turnings. I would suggest getting a copy of his DVD *Finishing Secrets for Pens*. This DVD runs 113 minutes and, as far as I'm concerned, is the definitive work on how to finish pens using the most popular finishes. Russ discusses the properties of various finishes, application techniques, and the pros and cons of various finishes. The DVD can be ordered from www.woodturnerruss.com. My finish of choice is CA (cyanoacrylate) glue. Other finishes to investigate include lacquer, water born lacquer such as Enduro®, Waterlox® and other oil finishes, shellac, friction polishes, French polishes, and of course no finish at all. Waxes, although not a finish, are also popular and worth time to investigate.

PEN TURNING TIPS AND HINTS

This picture shows the stock live center that comes with most mini lathes. The point is not a sixty degree point. Our pen mandrels have a 60° dimple in the end where the live center mates with the mandrel. The mandrel will have a tendency to wobble when the stock live center is used.

This is a sixty degree live center used with metal cutting lathes. This live center's point fits perfectly into the end of a pen mandrel, eliminating any off center wobbling. This is one of the best tools for helping make our turned pens perfectly round. They are not expensive and are now available from most of our favorite woodturning and pen turning sources.

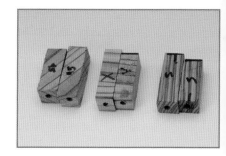

Pens made from the same stock can look totally different when cut at various angles to the grain. These blanks of Zebra wood are 45 degree cross grain cut on the left, cross grain cut on the center pair, and straight grain cut on the right. Pens from these three sets of blanks will look totally different and will add variety to pens made with blanks cut from the same stock.

After the blanks are cut, drilled, and the tubes glued in place, the ends of the blanks must be milled so the pen parts will mate with the ends of the turned barrels. This picture shows squaring the end of the pen blank with a pen mill. Pen mills are used in hand held drills and even drill presses. I consider the pen mill to be a hand tool, so I have made a handle for my pen mill. Squaring or milling the ends of the blanks can also be done with a jig and a disk or belt sander.

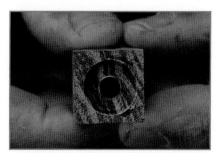

The squared end of a pen blank after using the pen mill. The milled ends of the blank are now perpendicular to the turning axis of the blank.

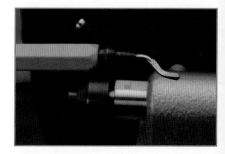

This is the deburring tool I use to remove the burr on the end of the brass tube created by the pen mill or disk sander. There are other styles of deburring tools, but this is the one I prefer.

The deburring tool in action.

Homemade acrylic pen blanks are shown. The coffee bean blank on the left was made by Eugene Soto. The next three moving to the right were made by Dawn Kizer (www.exoticblanks.com) and the shredded money blank and rattlesnake skin blank were made by the author. Homemade acrylic blanks are fun to make and much cheaper than purchasing.

Commercially available acrylic pen blanks purchased from various pen turning suppliers. Acrylics are fun to turn and can make very nice pens. I would suggest painting the "hole" in the blank to prevent the brass tube from showing through the thin acrylic of the finished pen. The author uses model airplane paint and chooses a color close to one of the colors in the blank. Different colors can change the character of the blank.

The Beall collet chuck, shown in this photo, and similar collet chucks use industry standard ER 32 collets from the metal working industry. These collet chucks were designed to accept ER32 collets which can be used to hold mandrels along with many different size materials and pen parts for shaping or modifying. Collets are available in both SAE and metric sizes. I used both the Beall collet chuck and the one sold by Penn State Industries while making the pens for this book. One major advantage of using collets is the amount of holding surface, which reduces or eliminates surface marring of the part being held.

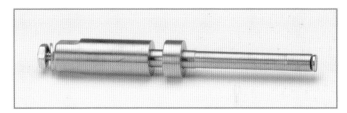

Closed end pen expanding mandrel used to hold a pen blank with a blind hole. A blind hole does not go completely through the blank. A closed end pen has no hardware on one or both ends of the pen. The baseball bat pen project in this book is an example of a close end pen. This closed end expanding pen mandrel in various sizes is available from www.arizonasilhouette.com

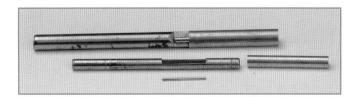

A pin chuck can also be used for holding blanks with blind holes. These two were made by the author in his shop. The blank with a glued-in tube is positioned over the slot and pin. When rotated toward the turner, the pin locks the blank in place for turning. A quick turn in the other direction will unlock the blank for removal from the chuck. Dedicated closed end pen mandrels, regardless of style or design, are tube size specific.

THE BASIC SLIMLINE PEN

T he first project of this book will be to make a Slimline pen as outlined in the instructions from the manufacturer. The set of components I chose to use is the comfort pen from Penn State Industries, item #PKCFFUNCH. This is a favorite of mine but I never use the rubber grip. I use this kit and similar kits because the clip style allows for making a larger cap barrel without interfering with the clip itself. The standard thin Slimline (black line clips) does not allow for making the upper barrel as large as I like to make them. Other 7mm or Slimline kits I use are the Trimline, item #PKXMCH, from PSI, the streamline 7mm flat top, item #BHW-019 from Arizona Silhouette, and the Biscayne flat top, item #AZSPK-24, also from Arizona Silhouette. Other similar kits may be available elsewhere. My plating of choice is chrome, although black or gold titanium and rhodium or platinum are also nice and wear well. The wood for Project #1 is maple burl.

The skills and steps for making a Slimline pen are shown here in Project #1. Most of these skills are needed to make the modified Slimline pens in subsequent projects and may or may not be shown but will be referenced.

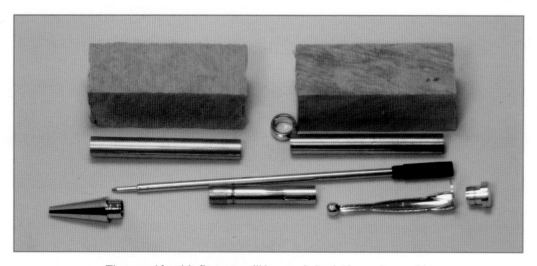

The wood for this first pen will be maple burl, shown here with the pen components. The tubes will be glued in place and the ends milled.

One of the maple burl blanks used in this first project is being turned round in preparation for drilling. The skew chisel is my "go to" tool, which I use almost exclusively from rough out to final turning. Learning to use the skew chisel is a skill well worth the time spent to master. Most of my sanding starts at 320 grit because of the smooth surface left after using the skew chisel. I do use different sizes of skew chisels. I also use a rough out gouge or carbide tipped tools from time to time. I do change tools as I deem necessary, depending upon turning conditions and the way the wood is responding.

The blank has been turned round to a diameter of approximately 3/4". The blank is being held using the Beall collet chuck and the 3/4" collet. If the diameter of the rounded blank is consistent from one end to the other, the blank will turn true with no wobble. Some alignment with the live center may be needed.

The drilling has started using a letter J bit held in a Jacobs chuck installed in the tailstock. I like the size of the hole made by the letter J bit better than the 7mm or other size bits that are suggested for Slimline pens.

The second blank section for this first pen project is being drilled. Drill in about 1/2", then retract the bit to eject the drilling chip.

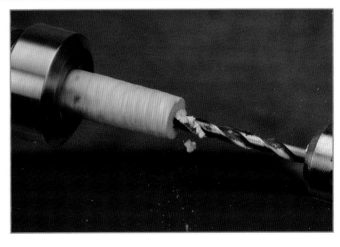

This picture shows holding the blank for drilling using a standard scroll chuck with pin jaws. Other styles of jaws can be used and dedicated pen blank drilling chucks are also available. Using other style chucks may or may not require the blanks to be rounded prior to drilling.

Square blanks, as well as rounded ones, can be held in the pin jaws of a scroll chuck

Drilling pen blanks can be done on a drill press, although I find drilling on the lathe to be much more accurate than using a drill press. Drilling on the lathe can save the price of a drill press or save on shop space if space is short and a drill press is not needed for other shop work. To drill on the lathe, a Jacobs chuck is needed along with a way to hold the pen blank. Most any scroll chuck can be used. I use a scroll chuck with pin jaws and I also use the collet chucks mentioned earlier.
To use the collet chuck, I turn the blank to a diameter of 3/4" and use the 3/4" collet to hold the blank. Drilling this way is very accurate. When using my scroll chuck, I leave the blank square. A dedicated chuck for holding pen blanks for drilling on the lathe is available from Penn State Industries.

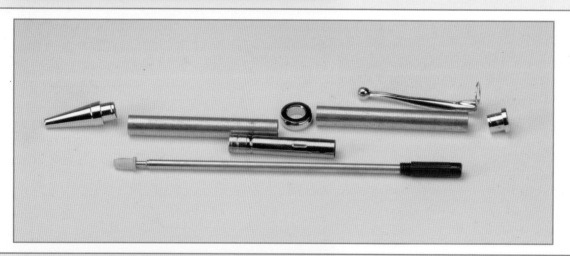

Typical parts included in a Slimline pen kit. Center band sizes vary from one Slimline kit to another.

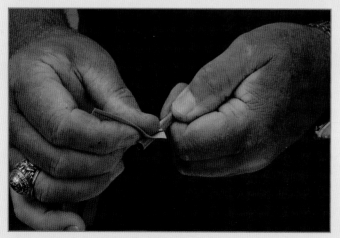

Now that the blanks are drilled, the tubes need to be glued into place. Scuff the tubes with sandpaper. This cleans the tube and the scuffed surface of the tube gives the glue a better surface with which to bond.

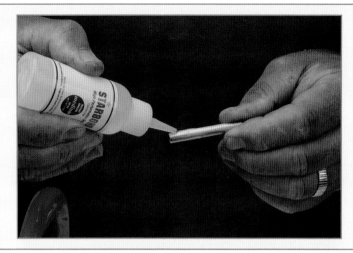

Cyanoacrylate glue, or CA glue, is being applied to the tube in preparation for gluing the tube into the drilled pen blank. My glue of choice is five minute two part epoxy when gluing tubes for one or two kits. When gluing tubes for several kits, I use thirty minute two part epoxy. CA glue was used for the photo shoot because of its fast set time.

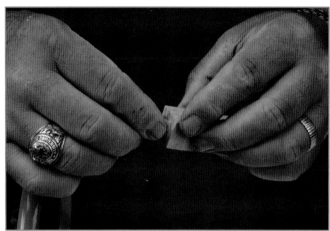

Insert the tube while twisting the tube in the blank to help disperse the glue. Good glue coverage is important for a satisfactory glue job. I also plug the hole in the brass tube entering the blank's hole, first, to help push the glue through the hole and, second, to keep glue from entering the tube. I use dental base plate wax, which I purchase from a local dental lab. Base plate wax is also available from Arizona Silhouette and from Internet sources.

The initial turning of one of the blanks for this pen. I turn one blank at a time mounted on the mandrel. Notice the bushings on each end of the blank and the brass nut holding the parts snug. The tail stock holds the mandrel in place and supports it also.

The brass nut and the tail stock are often over-tightened producing out of round pens. If the brass nut is too tight, the blank and brass tube may bow just a little. If the tail stock is too tight, the mandrel may bow, also contributing to out of round pens. If both are over-tightened, the possible out of roundness is compounded. Tighten the nut just enough to hold the blank secure during turning. Tighten the tail stock quill just enough to spin the live center and support the end of the mandrel.

Shaping the pen barrel continues. This will be the lower barrel. I normally shape from the center to each end of the blank to avoid tear out on the ends of the blank.

Shaping toward the other end of the blank. The nib end is on the left and the center band end is to the right. I always place the nib to the headstock end of my lathe and the clip end of the other barrel toward the live center.

The lower barrel close to its finished size. Shaping will continue.

The desired dimensions of the blank are being approached slowly. This blank is the lower barrel with the nib end on the left. I turn pens with the nib end next to the headstock and the clip end next to the tailstock.

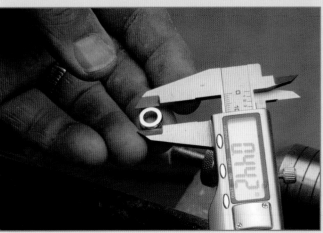

The center band is being measured using callipers so its diameter can be matched with the diameter of the pen blank. Bushings are used for holding the blanks on the mandrel and to give a close approximation to the final diameters. I use calipers to measure and help me match the ends of the blanks to the actual pen parts on each pen I make.

Checking the ends of the blank against the measurements from the kit parts ... I will slowly continue turning to meet the needed dimensions.

Final size is close. Just a little more turning and measuring and I will have the turning of this blank completed. One final pass with the skew and the blank is ready for sanding.

The pen barrel is now at the correct size. Mastering and using the skew chisel produces a pen barrel that is very smooth. This allows sanding to start at 320 grit sandpaper rather than starting with a lower grit.

Sanding is very important for the finish of the pen. The finish will be only as good as the surface on which it is applied. This is true for all finishes. Start sanding at the appropriate grit and progress through the grits without skipping any. Typical sanding would start at 220 grit then progress to 320, 400, 600 grits, and further if desired. I stop at 600 grit and then use Micro Mesh®.
Be sure to stop and sand lengthwise between grits to remove any radial sanding scratches. Also, clean the blank of any sanding dust prior to using the next grade of sandpaper. Just one piece of 320 grit abrasive carried over to sanding with a higher grit will leave 320 grit scratches and sanding will not be effective.

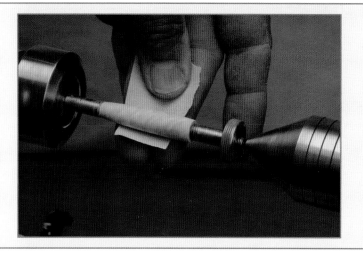

The bottom half of the pen is now turned to size and sanded smooth. It is ready to be finished. We will discuss finishes later in the book.

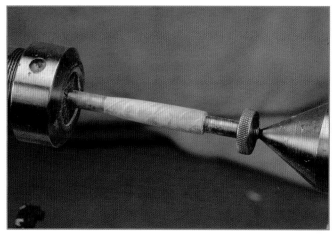

The upper blank is being rough turned with a rough out gouge. Normally I use a skew chisel, but I decided to use multiple tools for the book. We should each use the tool or tools that we have mastered. I have discovered that one of my bowl gouges with a fingernail grind works nicely when I turn certain burl pen blanks or cross cut ones.

Several times during the turning of a pen blank I stop the lathe, loosen the brass nut, and rotate the blank 1/4 turn or so. This rotation will help keep the blank nice and round. I turn one blank at a time on a short mandrel to help keep my pens round.

The upper barrel is now at the final diameters on the ends. Shaping between the ends is completed. Measurements were taken with calipers as noted above.

A final shaping and blending using the skew to get the desired final shape.

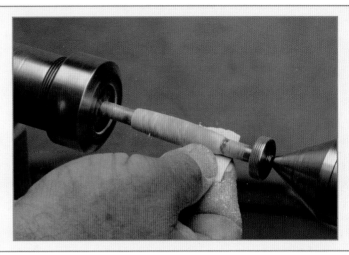

The blank is being sanded in preparation for applying a finish. Do not over sand!

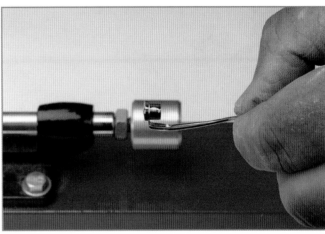

The finial has been inserted into the clip ring and is ready for being pressed into place in the end of the upper barrel.

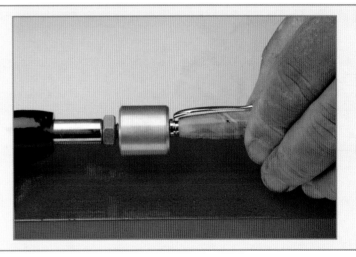

The finial has been inserted into the clip and is being pressed into place using a standard pen press. Other ways for pressing pen parts into place are possible. An arbor press is a popular alternative.

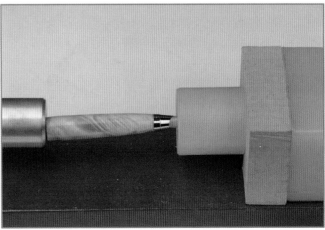

The pen tip is being pressed into place on the lower barrel.

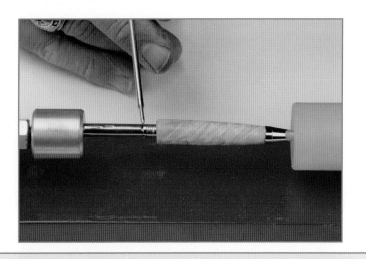

The transmission, or twist mechanism, is being pressed into place. The mechanism has a reference mark indicating how deep it should be seated. It is for reference only. Press, install the refill and check the refill for proper positioning of the tip when in the writing position. Continue to press and check until the proper position is achieved ...

For Slimline pen kits, the length from the tip of the nib to the end of the transmission is 3.95". Varying the length of the lower barrel does not change this measurement. In later projects the lower barrel's length will be longer or shorter than the standard length. Remember: 3.95".

The assembled pen made to the specs of the instructions for this particular Slimline. The kit is the Penn State Industries comfort pen, but the rubber grip was not used.

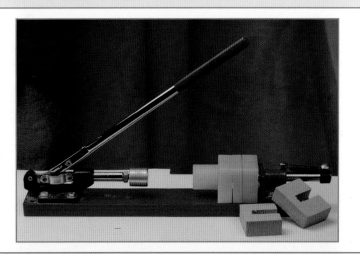

The pen press I use has spacers for adjusting the spacing between the two rams. I have made a few extra spacers from various widths of plywood and medium density fiberboard. No more tightening and loosening the hand nut to change the ram position.

Various Slimline pens made according to the manufacturer's instructions. Materials: left to right: Zebra Pattern Italian Resin from Exotic Blanks; Dyed Stabilized Curly Maple; Coffee Bean blanks by Eugene Soto; Lava Flow commercial resin from Craft Supplies; Rattlesnake under acrylic by Don Ward; Afzelia; Stabilized Buckeye Burl; and homemade polyester resin dyed black, made by Don Ward.

THE DON LINE

The Don Line pen is my adaptation of a pen made by Russ Fairfield. Russ called it the Russ Line. This modified Slimline has a longer, lower barrel than the standard length. The upper barrel's length is the standard length for the Slimline pen. But, its diameter is larger than the diameter of the lower barrel. Russ burned rings on the end of the upper barrel. My adaptation uses a thin slice of contrasting wood, acrylic, antler, or other material on the end of the upper barrel where the center band would normally be. Calling this pen the Don Line was suggested by Russ himself. Rest in Peace, my friend.

This photo shows the various center band materials I use. I am constantly on the lookout for new materials that can be used. The materials are, from left to right, top row: aluminum drink can; African blackwood slices; and plastic door sign stock. Bottom row left to right: guitar pick guard; credit card slices; soft drink bottle caps.

NOTE: Be careful when drilling some of these materials. Hold them securely to the drill press table on a waste block. They can suddenly lock onto the drill bit and become square blades. The aluminum can sections are as sharp as razor blades. I know this from personal experience.

The face of the center band slice that will glue to the pen blank needs to be scuffed with sandpaper for better glue adhesion. The wooden slices need to be squared with a pen mill. I drill the blank first. Then I place a tube over the pen mill shaft and square the end of the drilled blank. I then slice off a slice on the band saw. Use the pen mill and square the end of the blank again. Square the end of the blank and slice off another. The hole will need to be drilled deeper after a few slices are removed from the blank.

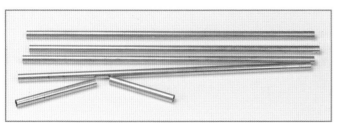

Many of the modified Slimline pens I make have one or both barrels longer than standard Slimline barrel lengths. I purchase 7mm brass tubes in 10" lengths and cutoff tube sections as needed. I use a micro-hacksaw with a small blade I buy from Hobby Lobby to cut the tubes. Harbor Freight also sells a small cutoff saw that is good to use for cutting brass tubes.

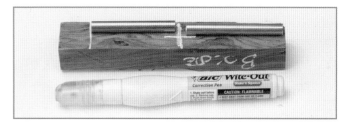

The blank for project #2 has been marked for sawing into sections. I use a BIC™ Wite-Out correction fluid pen for writing on pen blanks. The white is easy to see and does not soak into the wood fibers as an ink marker may do. The cross mark on the center cutting line will help me to keep the blanks oriented with the grain patterns matching. The wood species is bocote.

The blank for the upper barrel has been drilled and the tube glued into place. The blank is mounted on the lathe and is being rounded and shaped prior to the center band being glued onto the end.

The end where the slice of center band material is to be placed needs to be smaller than the pen mill's footprint on the accent band. Some pen mill's cutter heads have 1/2" diameters and others have 3/4" diameters. The milled side of the accent piece is shown and the pen mill's footprint is visible.

A 1/8" parting tool will be used to remove a section of the pen blank. It will be replaced with the African blackwood accent piece. Remove enough wood for the thickness of the blackwood accent slice being used. If the slice is thicker than the section being replaced, it can be milled down to the tube after it is glued into place.

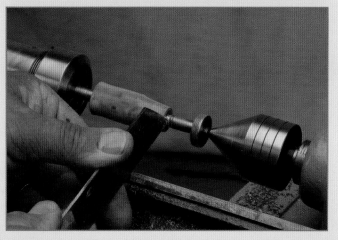

Wood removal is completed and the new end of the wood blank is squared to the tube and flat. This will insure a perfect fit between the blank and the blackwood slice.

The wooden slice is test fitted prior to gluing.

CA glue is applied to the milled surface of the slice of African blackwood.

Place the accent piece onto the exposed brass tube end and against the end of the pen blank. Hold the band tightly in place as the glue sets. I use medium or thick cyanoacrylate glue for this. A quick shot of accelerator will help the glue set quicker. Use a pen mill to square the other end of the accent band. Thicker CA glue gives more working time.

The accent band is in place, ready to be turned with the blank. A similar pen to project #2 is shown for comparison.

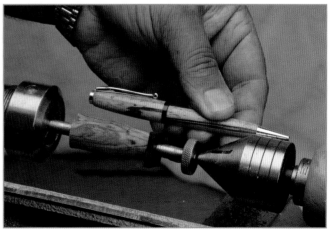

Start turning the upper barrel by first rounding the accent band. Turn the accent band to the same as the blank to which it is attached. Continue to shape the upper barrel using your favorite tool.

I have now switched to my favorite tool, the skew chisel, for final turning and shaping.

The upper barrel and accent band are complete and ready for sanding and finishing. For the kit I am using, the diameter of the upper barrel needs to be 1/2" or less close to the center. Larger diameters will cause the clip to touch the wood and not allow the pen to fit into a shirt pocket properly. This dimension will vary between Slimline kits from different manufacturers.

The lower barrel is now being turned and shaped. My design for this pen calls for the end that meets the upper barrel at the center to have a diameter smaller than the end of the upper barrel. Notice the dimensions in the pen at the beginning of this project. But, the interface where the two barrels meet can be the same diameter. To make them the same, I would suggest that both barrels be placed on the mandrel so they meet at the center. The final shaping can be done, seeing the pen's shape taking place.

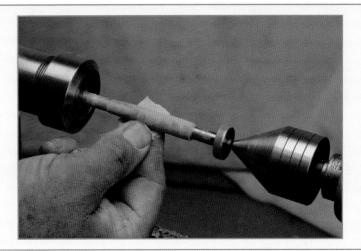

Sanding is done in preparation for applying the finish.

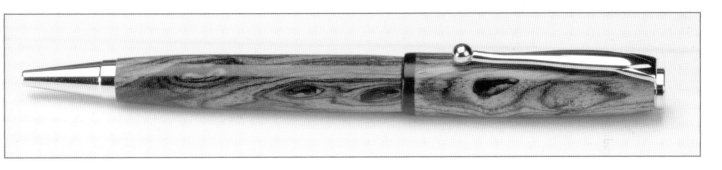

The assembled pen made to the specs of the instructions for this particular Slimline. The kit is the Penn State Industries comfort pen, but the rubber grip was not used.

With the longer lower tube, the transmission needs to be pressed in beyond the normal guide mark so the pen tip will clear the nib. The overall dimension from nib to end of transmission is 3.95". This length has worked well for my Slimline modifications whether the lower barrel is longer or not. But, as always, I slowly press the transmission close to its final placement, then check the refill by placing it in the pen and activating. Press in the transmission a little at a time until the desired refill tip exposure is reached.

I use a press block, as shown here, to make pressing in the transmission quick and accurate.

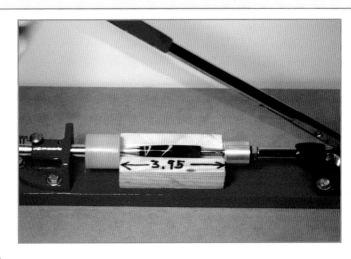

Center Band or Accent Band Materials

I have discovered several materials for use as accent rings, as shown in the previous pen project. These accent bands can be placed anywhere on the pen. Some common places include the ends of the barrel(s) or between the ends. When placed between the ends of the barrels (in the pen body) they can be placed perpendicular to the tubes or the blank can be cut at an angle and the band glued in place between the two pieces. Be sure all mating surfaces are flat so no gap is left when all is glued back together. Several accent bands can be used on the same pen, using the same accent band material or mixing them.

Wood: Wood is one material that is readily available to pen turners. Slice those unused pen blank ends and use them as accent bands. Prepare them as outlined in project #2. African blackwood is a favorite of mine. Pick a wood that compliments or contrasts with the main wood used for the pen.

Acrylics: Acrylic pen blank cutoffs are another excellent source for accent band material. I keep black acrylic acetate blanks for using as accent bands. Acrylic acetate is also one of my favorite acrylic materials.

Guitar Pick Guard: One of the popular and often used materials is the guitar pick guard. Pick guards are available in several color combinations. It is often made with layers of different colors laminated together. For our use, we are interested in the colored layers as they appear when looking at the edge of the material. The two surfaces are usually black and some other nice color or pattern that will be exposed when used on a guitar. I glue the black surface to the blank and leave the nice surface exposed on the end of the blank. Pick guard is available from suppliers who sell guitar-making materials, but other sources that meet pen turners' needs are available. Several pen kit suppliers sell pick guard already cut into 1" strips that are usually 6" long. Cut them into squares and drill a 7mm hole in the center and they are ready to use. Be careful!

Credit Cards and Hotel Key Cards: These cards make excellent accent bands. I destroy the portion of a credit card with the account numbers and use the other portion. Cut into squares, drill the hole and glue in place. The only negative that I have found is they mostly come in white, although a few can be found in dark colors.

Door Name Sign Material: Take a look at the name sign on your office door. Or the one on the little wooden name sign holder on your desk … or someone else's door. That material is really close to guitar pick guard material. Scrap pieces can often be obtained from the sign shops that make these signs. The laser engraving and trophy shop where I have pens engraved is my source for this material. Instead of tossing his scrap into the trash, my engraver saves it for me.

Drink Bottle Caps: These caps come in several colors. They are readily available and easy to use. Remove the seal on the inside or under side, sand to roughen the surface, drill, and glue into place.

Aluminum Drink Can Slices: I often cut 1" squares from aluminum drink cans and add them to other materials. For example, sandwich a slice of African blackwood between two of these thin aluminum slices or sandwich a slice of aluminum between two wood slices. More than one slice can be used to make the aluminum a little thicker. Both sides of the center slice of wood or other material need to be flat and squared to the hole so no gaps form when gluing the materials together. Thin aluminum sheet material can be used if available. Brass is also a possibility. Often brass washers can be found in the plumbing department of hardware or home center stores. Both aluminum and brass can be turned with HSS steel wood turning tools. I have made pens from aluminum bar stock using my wood turning tools. Aluminum grades that have worked well for me are 6061 or 7075. I would not suggest using aluminum bar stock from the local hardware store. It is often too hard an aluminum alloy to work well for this purpose.

Other Materials: Be creative! Keep your eyes open! Materials for use as accent rings are all around. Any thin plastic or soft metal can be used as well as those mentioned above. You will soon begin to look at materials normally tossed in the trash in a new light.

A green drink bottle cap has been cleaned and a 7mm hole drilled in the center. CA glue is applied to the surface around the hole.

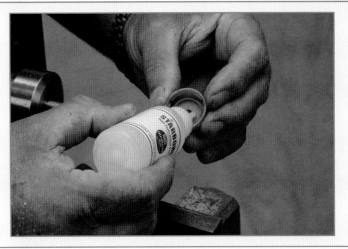

A wooden barrel has been prepared to accept the bottle cap. CA glue accelerator is sprayed onto the end of the blank that will receive the bottle cap.

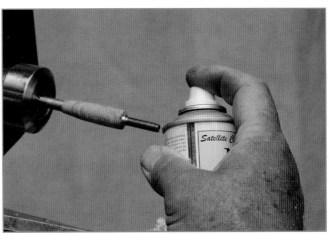

The cap has been positioned in place and held there long enough for the CA glue to set. A bushing and the brass nut are in place and the cap is now ready to be turned.

The cap is being turned using a skew chisel. I use the very end of the skew to cut off the part of the cap that will not be used. Then the portion glued to the pen blank is turned to the same size as the pen blank. After gluing and turning, the process is the same as used on the wooden accent band previously.

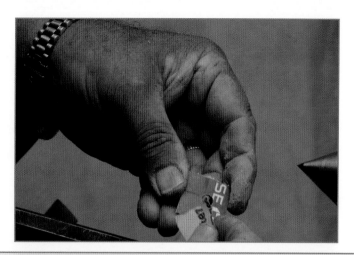

The next accent ring material is a section of credit card or hotel key card. A 1" square is cut and a 7mm hole drilled. The surface mating to the pen blank has been sanded to allow the glue to hold better.

CA glue has been applied to the card. Accelerator has been sprayed to the prepared blank. The card slice will be positioned on the end of the blank as before and held in place long enough for the glue to set.

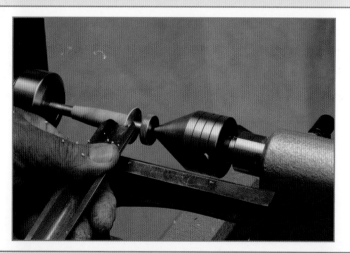

The card slice is being turned to the same dimension. The rough out gouge works well for all of these accent band materials. A skew used for a peeling cut also works well.

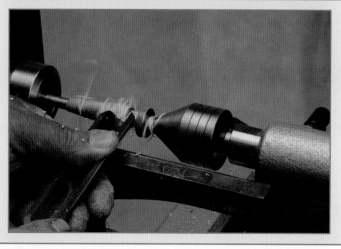

Plastics, pick guard material, credit cards, and other similar materials will tend to produce ribbons off the tools in unbroken strings and wrap around the pen blank. Stopping to remove the wound on material may be necessary.

The credit card accent band completed.

The credit card band is being parted off to make ready for the next material to be glued into place.

A slice of guitar pick guard, with the hole drilled, is ready to be glued into place. The layers are black-white-black and will be visible later.

The slice of pick guard is being rounded to size with a rough out gouge. The rough out gouge is my tool of choice for taking these slices down to the size of the blank. Then I change back to the skew chisel.

Here is the completed pen barrel with the slice of pick guard.

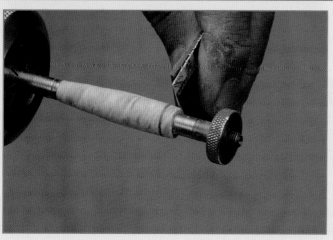

This next center band will be made from a slice of red and blue door sign material with a slice of credit card or hotel key card sandwiched between them. The three slices are held next to the blank and the blank is marked to show where to remove the wood.

Use a parting tool and remove the wood from the mark to the end of the blank all the way to the brass tube. Glue on the three slices as previously done with CA glue between the slices. Using thick CA glue will provide more working time to get glue between each slice. Glue them one at a time and press together to make the space between the slices as tight as possible.

The three section center band is being rounded with the rough out gouge.

The red, white, and blue center band is taking shape. Once again, notice the strings of plastic material wrapping around the mandrel. I stop often to clean off this material.

Now the material has begun to collect in the flute of my rough out gouge.

The three color band is completed and the blank is ready to be sanded and finished. The lathe is still spinning.

Here is a look at the red, white and blue laminated center band with the lathe off and all debris cleared.

This picture shows a black bottle cap glued onto the end after the wood has been removed to the brass tube. Turning the cap has begun.

This bottle cap center band will be turned with a skew chisel used in a scraping mode.

The center band is getting close to final size.

The completed bottle cap center band is shown. Notice the strings of material wrapped around the mandrel and blank. Bottle caps tend to produce long strings that will wrap. All plastic materials behave differently when used for center bands.

A small skew chisel is being used to cut shallow rings into the blank which will be darkened, or burned. Wire is the most popular material to use for burning these rings. The skew cut rings will keep the wire from skating up the blank.

A second ring is being cut. I like to cut three rings and keep them equally spaced.

Having no wire on hand I used the corner of a pen blank to create the friction to burn the rings. The rings need to be burned a little darker. The burned rings are wider than I wanted but when I sand they will get smaller and only the burned portion in the groove will be left.

One of my favorite uses of these slices of various materials is to place a 1/8" slice of wood on both ends of the upper barrel. My "go to" wood for this is African blackwood. I like the really black blanks with no sapwood. Black compliments most any other wood and most acrylics. The black acrylic acetate mentioned previously is also a favorite.

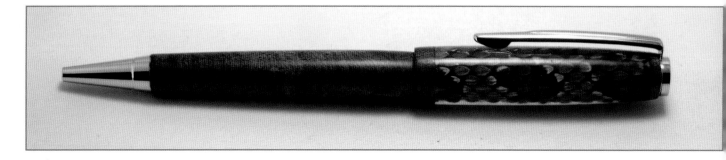

A Slimline pen with the upper barrel made from prairie rattle snake skin encapsulated in polyester resin and wooden slices sandwiching the snake skin section. The wood is local Texas mesquite.

I make my own rattlesnake skin blanks and I often apply this two slice treatment to the Slimline pens I make with wood on the bottom and a snake skin blank for the cap barrel. The cap barrel will have slices of the wood used on the bottom barrel on each end of the cap. A band saw used to cut these slices makes this chore quite simple. I will now show how the slices can be made using the lathe.

An African blackwood blank is in the pin jaws of my scroll chuck and a 7mm hole is being drilled. Drilling is being done with a Jacobs chuck in the tail stock and drilled on the lathe.

After the hole is drilled, the end of the blank is squared. I placed a 7mm tube on the pen mill pilot shaft and squared the end of the blank as usual.

A parting tool is used to part off a slice of the desired thickness. In this case the slice will be just a little over 1/8" thick.

The slice was just parted off but the camera did not catch it as it fell. Use the parting tool to face off the end of the blank then square the end using the pen mill.

The second slice is almost off. Put them both aside for use on the ends of a snake skin blank.

A snake skin blank is on the mandrel and turning has started. Once again, the skew chisel is my favorite tool and I use one almost exclusively. I do find the rough out gouge to be a bit aggressive, for me at least, on most acrylics and plastics. Spindle gouges can also be aggressive when used on plastics.

Rough turning continues with the skew chisel.

Once round, I changed to a rough out gouge. Not everyone finds the skew chisel to be a friendly tool. The rough out gouge needs to be sharp. Taking light cuts is best. Go slowly!

I have changed to a negative rake round nose scraper. I sometimes use the scraper to make the last few cuts. Some pen turners use a scraper almost exclusively for acrylics and plastics.

The 1/8" parting tool is used to remove material from both ends of the rattlesnake blank. Remove the material down to the brass tube. Make sure the new ends of the blank are as flat as possible, parallel to each other and perpendicular to the tubes. This is actually easy to do with a parting tool. Practice first on a waste blank.

Applying the bands is the same on every project. Use CA glue on the barrel, and accelerator on the band, hold the two together until they set. It won't take long. Glue the wooden slices onto both ends. Now you are ready to mount and round those bands. The thickness of the bands is a matter of personal taste. Make them as thick or thin as you wish.

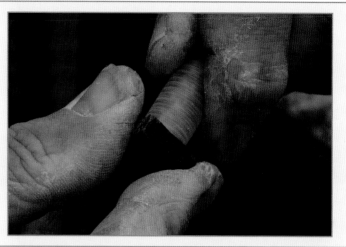

The slices can be sanded on a disk sander until they are just proud of the ends of the brass tube. Then the wooden ends need to be milled with a pen mill to square the ends as normal. Use your method of squaring.

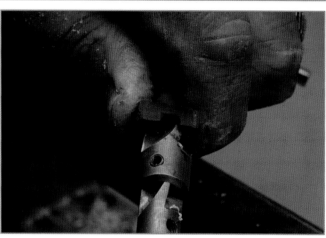

The blank is now on the mandrel ready for turning. The wooden ends will be rounded as we have previously done.

The wooden ends are being rounded using one of my skews. The rough out gouge can also be used. Use the tool with which you are most comfortable.

Final turning of the snake skin blank with wooden slices on the ends is taking place. Now is the time to decide the orientation of the snake skin scales. I think pointing toward the writing end is the most pleasing but the choice is a personal one.

I start sanding at 320 grit then move to 400 grit and then 600 grit. I then use MicroMesh™ and buff with a buffing compound. My normal buffing is done with NOVUS™ #3 and #2. Be sure to clean the sanding dust between grits and sand lengthwise to remove the circular sanding marks.

I am sanding with one of the MicroMesh™ pads. There are nine pads starting at 1500 and ending at 12000. The MicroMesh™ grit numbers are not equivalent to sandpaper.

The sanding is complete. How I polish acrylics and my snake skin blanks will be shown in a finished version of this pen later.

VARIATION ON THE DON LINE

This project is basically the Don Line made in project #2. The variation will be moving the accent band away from the end of the cap and placing it between the center end of the blank and the clip. I like to place it just below the clip.

The accent ring will be moved toward the clip and just below the end of the clip. I have decided where to slice the cap barrel and made the cut on my band saw. The tubes have been glued in place on the two larger blank sections. The slice will be glued later. Note the guide marks. These help keep the wood grain aligned among the pieces. The lower barrel is again longer than normal. Refer to Project #2. A similar pen is shown.

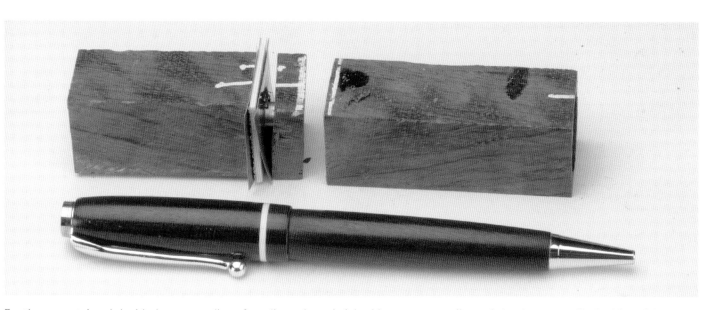

For the accent ring, I decided to use a slice of credit card sandwiched between two slices of aluminum can. Both sides of the small wooden section need to be squared with a pen mill as shown previously.

Turn the blank round. I have the black slice as a spacer over the end of the tube that is exposed. The blackwood slice is not glued and allows the bushing to hold the blank. It will be removed and discarded later.

It is really important to get the end where the pieces will be glued together turned down below the size of the pen mill's footprint. That way the laminated pieces will fit properly. Measure to make sure you have gone below the edge of the pen mill's footprint. Measure the pen mill first, and then the rounded wood. The blackwood slice has been removed.

I had to part off a little extra wood to make sure we have room for the band and aluminum slices and to insure that the end of the pen blank is nice and square, perpendicular to the brass center tube. A pen mill cannot be used here.

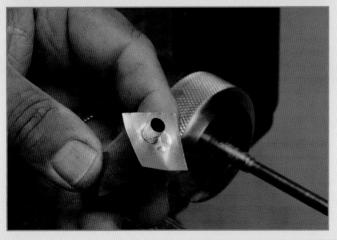

Loosely glue the three layers of the center band/accent ring together and to the wood. I used thick CA to give me more working time, but two part epoxy can be used for even more working time.

Firmly hold the wood and bands together as the glue sets. A little accelerator may be used. If epoxy is used to glue the pieces, then some form of clamp needs to be used to hold them until the epoxy cures. I often use a clamp, even with CA, and use no accelerator.

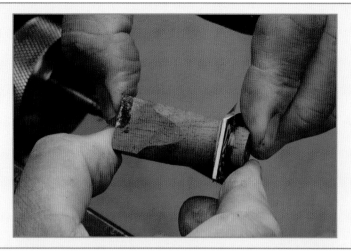

This end may need squaring again just to remove some wood to make the end of the blank even with the brass tube.

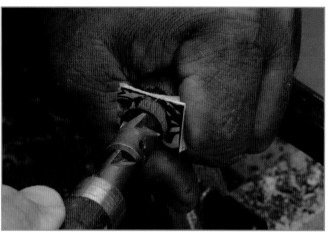

The accent ring is being turned to the same diameter as the blank. We have done this before.

Continue to shape the upper barrel with the rough out gouge. The clip end is on the right.

The blank is close to its final shape and size. A bit more refining and shaping is needed. For the kit I'm using, the tops need to be in the .52 inch diameter range or a bit smaller. If the center of the top barrel is too big, it hits the center of the clip and interferes with it going into a shirt pocket. Different kits will have different diameters. Check the kit you are using and adjust your measurements appropriately.

Sanding, as discussed earlier, getting ready for the finish to be applied.

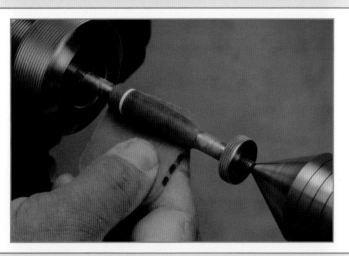

MicroMesh™ being used on the blank after 600 grit sandpaper. The blank has had a small amount of WATCO™ Danish Oil, medium walnut, applied. The oil slightly darkens the wood and makes the grain look much nicer. A CA glue finish has been used.

The upper barrel has been sanded and the finish applied.

Turning the lower barrel has begun. I normally turn from the center outward toward the ends to avoid any tear out or chipping from turning unsupported fibers.

The final shape of the lower barrel is forming, using a skew chisel. Making the bottom barrel is pretty straightforward. The only difference between this one and the standard Slimline is the length and the diameter at the center end. Sand and apply the finish.

Assemble as usual.
The assembled pen is
shown in this picture.

VARIATION II ON THE DON LINE

Matching Pen and Pencil Set

This project will show how to make a pen and pencil set based on the Don Line pen. The set will match as much as possible, or I should say as much as I can make them match. The pencil's overall length is the most critical so the pencil will be built first then the pen will be made to match.

The challenge for this pen will be making the blank for the pencil. The blank will have a length equal to the total length of the two tubes pressed onto the center band coupler. The coupler's center band feature will need to be removed or a single length of tube can be used. If using two tubes and the center band coupler, then the center band feature can be removed on the grinding wheel or on the lathe. The metal is brass and can be turned with HSS tools. I use the collet chuck and a parting tool. Using a single length of tube is much easier. If the two pencil tubes are used with the center band coupler I would suggest the tubes be glued to the coupler with a drop of CA glue. This will help keep the pencil from coming apart. The blank pieces for the pencil will be glued into a single piece later. This will also help add strength and keep the pencil together.

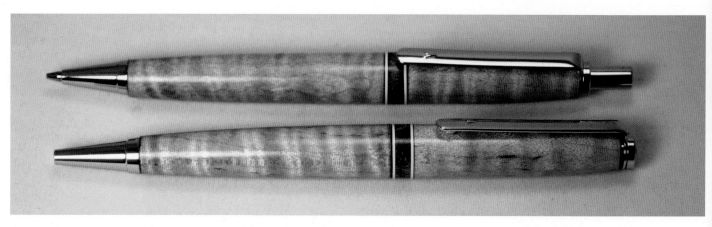

Here is a picture of a pen and pencil set similar to the set to be made in project #4.

The blanks have been cut to the same lengths as in the previous projects and will be adjusted to final length later. The top tubes are the pencil tubes and have been pressed onto the center coupler of the pencil. The center coupler needs to be ground down to the same size as the tube diameter so it will fit inside the drilled blank. Or, a 10" brass tube cut to the length of both tubes plus the exposed section of the coupler can be used. The wood blanks for both the pen and pencil are shown. I'm using figured walnut for this set.

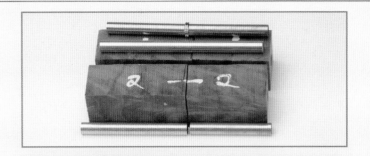

The pencil blanks have been placed on a mandrel but the tubes have not been glued in place. I will turn the blanks round concentrating on getting the center ends turned a bit smaller than my pen mill's footprint. This has been done before. Yes, a custom center band will be used.

Blanks for any pen can be turned without gluing in the tubes. The bushings will hold the wood when the brass nut is tightened. I do this often. If I don't like the looks of the wood, I can remove the tubes and try another pen blank.

The blanks on the tubes are being turned round with a rough out gouge but the brass tubes are not glued into place. We will glue the tubes later. The two ends at the center will need to be turned to a diameter just a bit smaller than my pen mill's footprint as we have done before. The blanks are touching at the center with no bushing.

Continue turning. Once the two center ends are small enough, they will need to be milled with the pen mill to insure the gluing will not produce gaps.

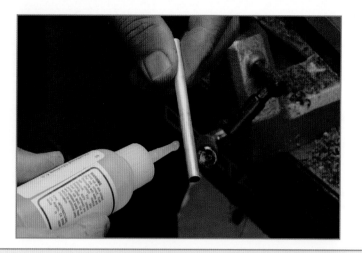

This tube is a single tube whose length is the same as the two pencil tubes, plus the exposed portion of the center band coupler. Using a single tube is easier, but using both tubes and the center band coupler works also. Remember, the center band feature needs to be reduced to the same diameter as the tube. The tube has been sanded and CA glue is being applied for gluing.

The two blanks are just a little longer than they need to be. I will glue both blanks onto the tube with the ends just a little proud of the tube ends. Milling will get them to the correct length. A slice of guitar pick guard will be used for a center band feature. The lower tube is longer than the upper tube as we did for projects 2 and 3.

The upper cap tube is glued into place and the pick guard slice is also glued using thick CA glue. When the glue has set, the lower barrel will be glued into place.

The lower barrel is now glued into place and the blank is being held tightly until the glue sets. I used medium CA for the lower tube so my hand will not need to be a clamp for long. Before placing on the mandrel, the ends of the glued blank need to be milled with the pen mill to square them and to get the blank to the proper length.

The pencil blank and pick guard slice are now ready to be turned.

The pencil blank is being turned. It is approaching its final shape and diameters.

I have changed to the skew for final shaping. The pencil can be seen taking shape. Now is the time to be looking and deciding on the final shape. Will the pen and pencil be simple bushing to bushing? Or, will they have a slight curve to them? Beads? Coves? Captive ring? Many designs are possible. Go with what you like and think looks good.

The pencil is completed and needs to have the finish applied. The writing end is on the right. The clip end is just a little larger than the clip ring and finial but the edge is rounded over to remove the sharp corner. The shape is larger in the center and tapers towards the ends. This is the shape I have settled on, but you can decide on the shape that best appeals to your taste and customers (if you sell your pens).

The pencil blank is completed and a CA glue finish applied. I use a coat of WATCO™ Danish Oil in medium walnut on most of the pens I make. The wood is darkened just a little and the grain really takes on character. Then the finish is applied. My finish of choice is CA glue but lacquer is another favorite. Now it is time to make the pen.

The pen's two sections will be made to match the pencil. The cap barrel is being matched to the pencil's cap barrel. The excess brass tube, if any is exposed after gluing the pick guard, will be removed.

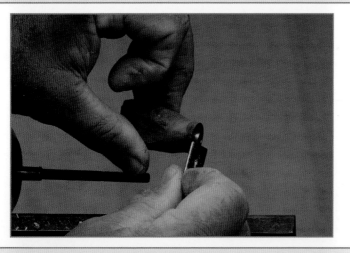

The cap barrel has the end at the center turned round to a diameter less than my pen mill's footprint. We have done this before and will be a standard step when using slices for accent bands. A section equal to the thickness of the guitar pick guard has been parted off and the end of the blank has been "milled" with the parting tool. The pick guard will now be glued in place as we have done previously.

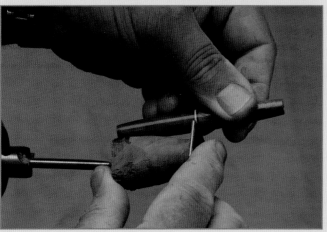

The cap barrel of the pen is now the same length as the cap barrel of the pencil.

The lower barrel for the pencil has the tube glued in place and its length tweaked so it is the same length as the pencil. Both blanks are on the mandrel. **NOTE:** The two blanks are NOT glued together like we did for the pencil. Turning them together will allow me to match the pen's shape to the shape of the pencil as closely as possible. Keep the pencil barrel close by for reference.

The two barrels are being turned to match the pencil's shape. It is easy to get the two ends mixed, so take note to keep the longer blank the lower barrel. *Yes*, I have mixed them up. Stay focused!

The pen is taking shape. Remember which end is the clip end and which is the writing end.

Once again, I have switched to the skew chisel for final shaping. A little more work is needed on the nib end … to the right. Remember which end is the nib and which is the clip!

The pick guard center band on pencil is .483" in diameter and pick guard center band on the pen is .524" in diameter. A little more work is needed. The pen and pencil should match in length, in center band placement, in diameters at various places along the barrels and in shape.

Turning is completed and sanding is next, followed with the finish. I stopped using the skew when the dimensions of the pen were just a couple of thousandths larger than needed. The last bit of material was removed during sanding.

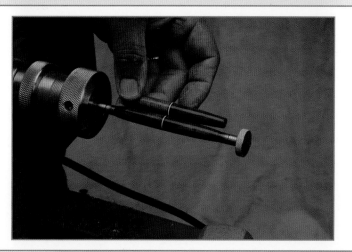

The pen's finish is the same as the pencil's finish. The two are shown for comparison. The pen is still on the mandrel. Assembly is next and is not difficult. Follow the printed instructions from the manufacturer for the pencil's assembly. Just remember, we have two barrels on the pencil glued together to make one barrel. The steps for pressing the center band coupler and the two tubes together has already been done. Assembly of the pencil has no surprises. Follow the instructions.

The finished pen and pencil set. They look really close. What a fun project!

HUNTER'S SPECIAL

Rifle Shell Pen

Over the last few years, several pen styles have become popular using various parts from rifle shells. Some pens use the entire rifle case, but use the pen kit nib. Others, as the one I will make next, use an actual bullet for the nib. Some designs use the butt section of the rifle case on the ends of the upper barrel. Once a rifle shell pen is made, the techniques learned can be used for making several designs. To keep with the theme of this book, I will use Slimline parts for the next project. But, the same techniques can be used with parts from kits that use the Parker® type refill as in the cigar pen or the Big Ben.

I use new shell cases, which do not have a primer. The location of the primer will be drilled out. I do not recommend using live ammo and taking the shells apart. Using live ammo is very dangerous. I suggest staying with either new rifle cases or used ones. I use new ones because once fired the neck expands and a bullet will not fit. The neck will need to be reduced in diameter so a rifle bullet can be pressed into place. This requires purchasing a tool for "necking down" the neck of an expended rifle casing. A new shell is ready for a bullet to be pressed into place. I also use the nickel or chrome-plated shells. I like the look better than brass, which will tarnish unless powder coated with clear. Some guys like the tarnished look of brass. I prefer the look of the nickel-plated shells and use chrome-plated pen parts.

The cap barrel can be made of several materials. Wood, antler, and acrylics are all excellent choices. I use a lot of antler, along with acrylics, in various camouflage patterns. Just think of it: a pen made for a young hunter using antler from the first deer along with the rifle case that was fired to bag the deer.

Several calibers can be used and I have made pens from some very large calibers by special request. My favorite calibers are the Winchester 280 Rem, Winchester 30-06 Spring, and the 25-06. 30 caliber shells are a good size to use. For the 280, a 7mm bullet is used and for the 30-06 a 30 caliber bullet is used. Once the process is learned, then other calibers can be used.

No special tooling is needed to make pens using rifle shell cases. I do use the collet chuck to hold the shell case and bullet for drilling. I also solder the brass tube into place in the shell case. If collet chucks are not available, then some method for holding these two parts for drilling must be devised. I have friends who make wooden collets and hold them with pin jaws on their scroll chucks. The parts must be held without marring during the drilling. The pens just don't look very good with the shell case and bullet scratched or dented from holding them for drilling. The following photographs show some ways to hold these rifle shell pen parts.

Homemade collets can be made from wood as shown in this photo. The hole is drilled the size needed and the slots were cut on a band saw. Similar wooden collets can be made for holding the lead bullet for drilling.

The wooden collet clamp, shell case inserted, for holding the collet against the shell. The collet is being held in a standard woodturning chuck with pin jaws. "The main disadvantage is getting the collet to run true in the chuck with no wobble." False. The more perfectly round the wooden collet is turned and the more dead center the hole is drilled, then the more true the collet will turn without wobbling. Some adjustment will be needed. **NOTE:** Be careful of the spinning hose clamp and keep fingers and hands out of harm's way.

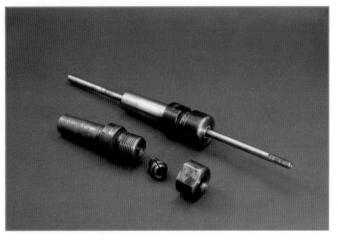

Two adjustable mandrels with MT2 (Morris Taper #2) arbors. One has the mandrel installed and the other has the parts disassembled. The collet can be used to hold bullets. Drilling or reaming the collet's hole to the correct size may be needed. The collet shown will hold one of the bullets I use. Another one had to be drilled out a bit larger.

The mandrel arbor is inserted into the lathe headstock's taper and is holding a bullet ready for drilling. A draw bar to safely hold the arbor in place is highly recommended.

Here is another solution. A hand held tap holder has a collet similar to the adjustable mandrel. The collet's hole is also the size of one of the bullets I use and possibly could be drilled larger to hold a different caliber. One problem is that these solutions only hold one size bullet.

The tap holder is being held in the same chuck used to hold the wooden collet shown previously. Holding the tap holder with no wobble is one of the downsides. But, it works.

Other homemade tools or improvised methods for holding the bullet and shell case are possible; the collet chucks like the Beall collet chuck or the one from PSI are by far the best. If making large numbers of these rifle shell/bullet pens is planned, then purchasing the collet chuck system and a set of collets is advisable. The PSI set comes with five collets and individual collets can be purchased as needed.

The first step is to drill the butt end of the shell case to accept the brass tube. These are new shell cases with no primer. If you have one with the primer, take it out. **If you have a live bullet … don't use it**. Taking a live bullet apart *can be quite dangerous*. The shell case is secured in a 15/32 collett.

The shell case is being drilled through the butt end. The primer slot serves to center the bit. The 7mm bit is .2756" and the letter J bit is .277". Either one will work but I drill mostly with the letter J bit. The OD (outer diameter) of the brass tubes can vary between manufactures or production runs. I measure brass tubes with calipers, then choose the drill bit that best fits. I do this with all kits, not just the Slimline kit. Often the bit I use is not the bit recommended in the manufacturer's instructions.

The hole is drilled and now the burr must be removed. Deburring tools are handy, but I use something I already have.

I use a tool with a square carbide cutter to remove the burr. A parting tool or the tip of a skew can also be used.

The next step is to drill the lead bullet to allow the pen's ink refill to move through it. Two bits are needed. Notice the refill. The larger bit is a 5/32" and will accommodate the larger diameter of the refill. The smaller bit is a 3/32" bit and will accommodate the smaller portion of the refill.

The larger bit will be used first and the smaller bit will be used to drill out the small end of the bullet. The hole in the bullet will be a stepped hole starting at the butt end with the larger bore then stepping down to the smaller bore for the last bit and out the tip of the bullet. The bullets I use are lead with copper jackets. Lead is difficult to drill because it is soft and has a low melting point. I have had the lead ball onto the drill bit and come out with the bit, leaving only a copper shell. I understand there is now a solid copper bullet, which should make drilling the bullet much easier. I have not looked for them but I will do so. I do not hunt, so this bullet and rifle shell lingo means little to me.

To help me decide how deep the first, larger bit should penetrate, I place the pen refill's tip and the bullet side by side. I try to place the writing tip where I think it should be when in the writing position. I make a mark on the bullet where the refill's diameter steps down to the smaller diameter. I then measure from the bullet's butt end to the mark. On this bullet, the measurement is about 3/4". Some tuning of the final drillings may be necessary.

Once again, I am using the collet chuck and a collet to hold the bullet for drilling. Starting from the back end of the lead bullet, I'm beginning to drill with the larger bit. I'm drilling about 3/4" deep for this 7mm 140 gr bullet. The drilling depth may vary as the bullet's length changes between calibers. When drilling, go slowly, no more than 1/4" or less at a time. You may need lubricating oil to keep from pulling the entire lead center out of the copper jacket.

The change has been made to the smaller bit and the smaller hole is drilled through the larger hole out the tip end of the bullet ... I hope! We will find out soon. The bullet can be turned around and the smaller bit can be drilled through the tip of the bullet.

I have not moved the bullet in the collet chuck, nor have I moved the Jacobs chuck. I just loosened the Jacobs chuck and swapped bits. I try not to do anything to get the bullet and drill bit out of line. I want the center line of both bits and the bullet to stay aligned. This will help the smaller bit to exit exactly on the center of the bullet's tip.

I use the carbide tool again to clean any burrs around the edge of the hole on the butt end. The bullet still has not been removed from the collet. I want to keep all holes and cuts on the bullet concentric.

The carbide tool is used to cut a tenon on the end of the bullet. The tenon's length should be small. A 1/16" long tenon is plenty, but a little longer is okay too. A parting tool can also be used. This tenon needs to have a diameter small enough for the brass tube to slip over it.

Test the brass tube's fit over the tenon. Turn and test until the tube just slips over the tenon.

It is now time to remove the bullet and see how the drilling went. Check the refill to see how far it protrudes from the end of the bullet. The writing tip needs to exit the hole and stop when the larger diameter section hits the smaller hole. The exact position of the tip's protrusion will be determined when we press the transmission in place. If the larger hole needs to be longer, then place the bullet back in the collet. Align the hole with the drill bit and make the hole a little longer. This can sometime be done by hand. Insert the bit and use the Jacobs chuck as a handle and turn the bit a revolution or two. Test again and adjust as needed.

The bullet has been reversed. Yes! The bit exited dead center on the bullet's tip. I used the carbide tool to clean the tip just a bit, making sure the end is nice and straight and square to the hole. Go lightly! Not much is needed.

After making a minor adjustment with the larger drill bit to accommodate the pen cartridge's shoulder, the fit was right. I use MicroMesh™ to clean and polish the copper bullet.

Drilling, adjusting, cleaning, deburring, and polishing are complete. The refill fits fine and the tip will extend exactly as we want it to. The bullet is ready to be pressed into the shell case.

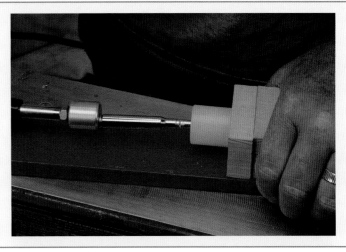

Use the pen press to press the lead bullet into the shell case. Be careful as the tolerances are very tight and it can be challenging to get the bullet to insert straight into the shell case. Stop pressing when the row of ribs around the bullet just disappear into the shell case. Press too far and the bullet will drop into the shell case.

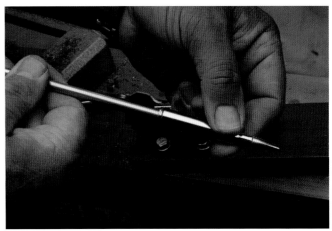

Next, insert the brass tube, making sure it fits over the tenon cut into the bullet's base. A small drop of CA glue can be used to help hold the tube in place. The long tube will be used as a handle while soldering the tube in place.

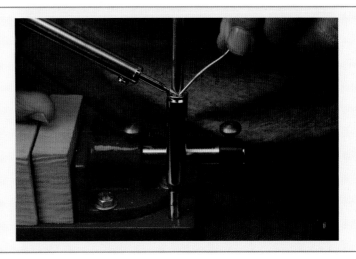

The brass tube is soldered in place. Use the proper solder and soldering paste. I use Oatey® silver solder and No. 95 tinning flux. They come packaged together and work fine for this soldering.

The soldering job is complete. Now a little clean up is needed. Most of the exposed brass tube has been removed. A small tubing cutter is handy for this job or a micro hack saw.

The shell case with the bullet and brass tube has been placed back in the collet chuck. A little clean up is needed.

Using the carbide tool I now remove excess tubing and excess solder from the end of the shell case. Be careful to not cut into the end of the case. I try not to get too much solder on the butt end of the shell case.

A little more careful clean up with the carbide tool.

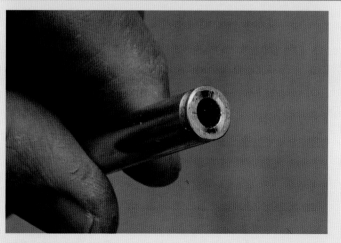

The shell case is now ready for the transmission to be seated in place. I must be careful to not press on the bullet as I would normally do had I used the kit's nib. We don't want the bullet to be pressed into the shell case.

The total length of the transmission from tip of the bullet to the end of the transmission needs to be 3.95". This is the standard length discussed earlier. To keep from pressing on the bullet itself I use a press block. The block is a section of pen blank drilled with a bit that is larger than the neck of the shell case but smaller than the shell case body. Placing the bullet end of the shell into the hole will allow the shoulder of the shell to rest against the end of the pen blank. The shoulder will take the force of the pen press instead of the bullet. The bit size I used to drill the hole in the half blank was a letter O bit. Measure the neck size and the shell case size and pick a bit between the two. Choose a bit closer to the neck size.

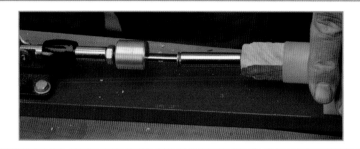

Insert the bullet end of the shell case into the hole in the half blank and position the transmission and then press the transmission into the brass tube. This is the same as we have done on previous projects. Remember: 3.95" ... stop short and check.

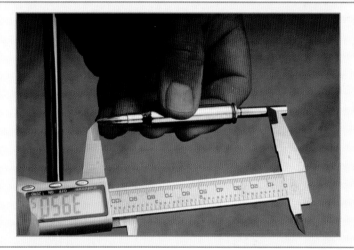

I have the caliper set to 3.95". The transmission needs to be pressed in a little further. As before, press and check until the total length from bullet tip to transmission end is 3.95". Or, use the press block gauge shown earlier.

The transmission is in place as well as the refill. Twisting the transmission shows the proper extension of the writing tip. Making the cap is next.

For the cap, I have chosen a camouflage blank. Antler is my normal material for the caps of these shell case pens. Making the cap is exactly the same as we have been doing. Measure the length needed, cut the blank, drill, and glue the tube into place. Mill the ends and mount on the mandrel. Using the collet chuck for holding the mandrel allows me to shorten the mandrel for turning one half blank.

The camouflage blank material and others made from similar plastics can be softer than most. Drilling can be problematic. The material heats and becomes very soft. Use water to cool the blank while drilling. Drill about 1/4", extract the bit, and repeat. Some testing using cut offs can help determine the softness of acrylic blanks.

A carbide tool with a square cutter is used to round the blank. Most any tool will work. Use your favorite. I am using a variety of tools for these projects to show that most any tool on the rack will work for pens.

Now I have switched to a carbide tool with a round cutter. The carbide tools I use are Easy Wood Tools™ easy rougher and easy finisher. This material is softer than many other acrylics or plastics, but turns easily. This round carbide tool, the Easy Wood Tools™ easy finisher, allows me to cut with a small tip section for more delicate work.

The camo cap is ready for sanding and polishing.

I'm using the PFK-1 Sanding Pads designed especially for resins and acrylics from www.bgartforms.com. The set of pads has 3 double-sided pads yielding 6 sanding grits. The yellow pad is 600 grit; the light green is 800 grit; orange 1500 grit; purple 2400 grit; light blue 4000 grit; and gray 12,000 grit. These are wet sanding pads.

The camo cap for the bullet pen is ready for the clip and finial to be pressed into place.

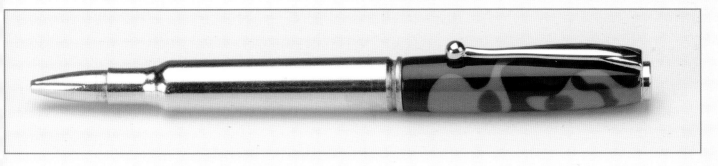

The completed pen using a 280 Remington shell case, a 7mm 140 gr copper clad bullet for the nib and an acrylic camo blank for the upper barrel. A fun project!

These two pens use two different calibers of shell cases. The top pen is a 308 caliber shell case plated in nickel. The cap is an acrylic in a horn pattern. The bottom pen is a 30-06 brass shell case and the cap is axis antler.

FINISHES FOR PENS

There are several types of finishes available for pen turners. A pen isn't completed until it is finished! The finish used on a pen can make a mediocre piece of wood become a fantastic pen or, on the contrary, can make a fantastic piece of wood become a mediocre pen. Each pen turner needs to decide what they want from a finish and learn to apply a product and apply it well. I do not pretend to be an expert on pen finishes. Take my previous advice and read what the late Russ Fairfield has to say about finishes for pens. His finishing information can be found at www.woodturnerruss.com.

Types of Finishes

1. Friction Polishes: Friction polishes such as Myland's™ High Build Friction Polish, HUT's™ Crystal Coat, Shellawax™, and similar friction polishes sold under various supplier's house brands are shellac based and seem to be the first finish we as pen turners use. Friction is the operative word in friction polishes. Friction from the applicator creates heat to evaporate the solvent and leaves the shellac behind. Friction polishes work great for items that are not handled frequently but, in my opinion, are not one of the better finishes for pens. Pens are used and handled. The pen will pick up oils, moisture, and dirt from our hands and friction polish finishes will soon become dull and will darken. Friction polishes have their fans and those who like them will use nothing else. Pens get a warm, woody feeling to them, a look I don't like, but that is just personal preference. A few mistakes made using friction polishes include the following: (1) Too much product is used for each layer. Less is more when building several layers to the shine depth desired. (2) Too little pressure producing a small amount of friction and too little heat to evaporate the solvent adequately is one of the major mistakes using friction polishes. Remember, they are called friction polishes for a reason. (3) Although the finish appears to be dry and hard after the last coat, friction polish needs a few hours to totally cure to optimum hardness. Ideally, the blanks should be left on the mandrel today and cure for 24 hours. Realistically, the blanks can be gently removed from the mandrel and placed on a dowel rod to be held for curing. (4) And, finally, friction polishes seem to produce their highest shine when applied over a base of some kind of sealer. Each brand of friction polish has a companion sanding sealer that, when used under the polish, will produce the best possible shine.

II. Lacquer-based friction polishes have become available. I have not used any, so I have no comments. But, lacquer-based friction polishes do deserve consideration if friction polishes are the finish of choice in your shop.

III. Lacquer is an excellent choice as a pen finish. I prefer a brushing lacquer diluted with an equal amount of lacquer thinner producing a 50-50 mix. I apply lacquer on the lathe with a soft cloth. I apply several coats, letting each layer dry before the next one is applied. Although lacquer dries fast, it cures slowly. Lacquer need up to a week or longer to totally cure depending on temperature and humidity. I often allow lacquer finished pens to cure for a minimum of two weeks. Once cured, lacquer can be buffed to a deep and lustrous shine. Mistakes using lacquer include too few layers and not allowing enough curing time prior to buffing. Water born lacquers, such as Enduro™, are also excellent choices and are gaining popularity. Pen blanks can also be dipped using lacquer, but that is another finish I have not investigated.

IV. Polyurethanes are also used by many pen turners for pen finishes. Brush on and spray on are both popular. Be sure to get polyurethane that is non-yellowing if polyurethane is used. I do not use polyurethane so I have no further comments.

V. Other finishes include Plexiglas™ dissolved in acetone. Those who use it call it plexitone. This is another finish I have not been interested in trying so I have no firsthand knowledge of it. The reports I have seen are that it produces a brilliant shine. Look on the shelves at the local woodworkers store and there will be many choices of various finishes. We could spend much of our time investigating finishes. I would rather be making pens than testing finishes. That is why I have settled on my finish of choice and have spent lots of time perfecting it. My finish of choice is CA glue with boiled linseed oil.

VI. CA glue is my choice for finishing a pen. I use it with boiled linseed oil, although it can be, and is, used alone. Those who use boiled linseed oil with CA glue are loyal and those who do not use CA with the oil are just as loyal to CA alone. I will not mention brand names, but I will say that I have used just about every brand out there and they all seem to perform just about the same … at least for me. What applicator is the best? This is a question that has as many answers as there are those who use CA glue as a pen finish. Well, maybe not that many. I use Bounty™ paper towels but others swear by other brands. Viva™ along with blue shop towels are other popular applicators. Here is a short list of applicator material that I have heard people use: (1) unwashed synthetic bath towel material, (2) synthetic packing peanuts, (3) the little baggies that our pen parts ship in, (4) synthetic batting material wrapped around a craft stick, (5) delrin strips, and (6) probably others I can't recall. The following is a step by step pictorial of how I use CA and boiled linseed oil as a finish for pens.

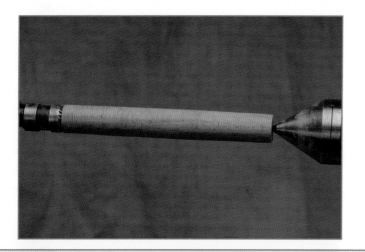

This piece of maple is sanded to 600 grit, sanding lengthwise between each grit and cleaning the dust off from each sanding before moving on to the next grade. After that I go through the nine grades of micro-mesh, from 1500 to 12,000 grit. Your finish is only as good as the surface to which it is being applied. This is the same treatment I would give any pen barrel before finishing.

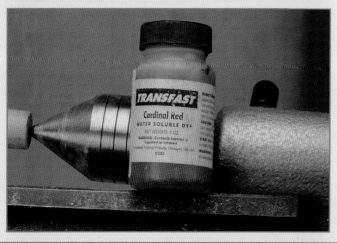

I'll be using water soluble aniline dye for staining the maple spindle. Aniline dye that dissolves in alcohol is also available. This dye comes in several colors. Any good woodworking store will have it. I do this to show that lighter woods can be dyed to produce some nice colors. I do not use dye on every pen.

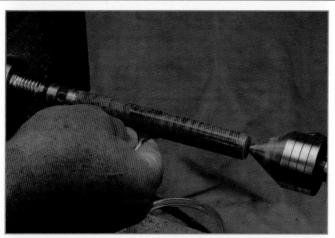

Apply the dye with a soft paper towel. The paper towel works as your brush.

The dye has been applied using two applications.

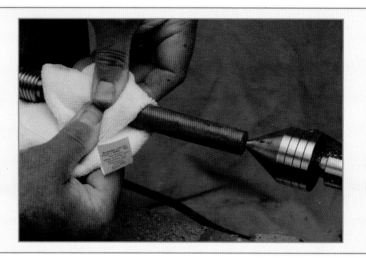

I'm using a microfiber cloth to smooth the grain while applying friction to produce heat to dry the water based dye. Water will raise the grain slightly and the microfiber cloth will smooth the surface.

I first apply a thin coat of WATCO™ Danish Oil in medium walnut. I use the Danish oil on almost every pen I make. It will darken the wood just a little and make the grain really stand out. I use a paper towel and lightly dry the oil surface.

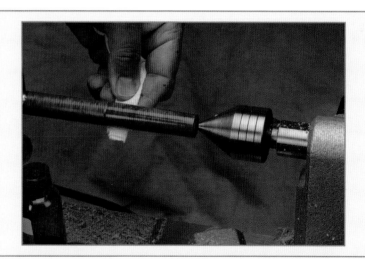

On the right half of this sample barrel I'm using boiled linseed oil and medium CA glue. A little oil, about two drops, is applied to the pen barrel, followed by a layer of CA glue.

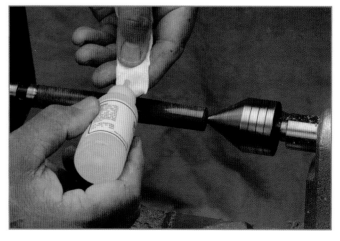

The CA glue is placed on a paper towel section folded over several times, then the CA glue is applied to the slowly spinning pen blank. I continue to move the paper towel back and forth until the glue is dry and no longer sticky. This is repeated for about 5 or 6 coats: oil, CA, oil, CA, etc.

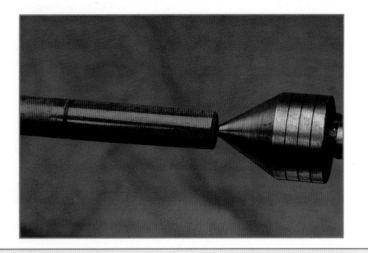

After several layers, the finish is complete and ready for sanding and buffing. I do not sand between layers. I rarely sand after the last coat, but sanding is sometimes needed to smooth out the surface.

I do use MicroMesh™ and sometimes I wet sand with it. Buffing is done using NOVUS™ Plastic Polish #3 and #2, but other buffing compounds are available and work well. Tripoli and white diamond are another favorite buffing compound duo. Sanding with 400 grit sandpaper is sometimes needed to smooth the surface. After the sandpaper, I either use MicroMesh™ or the double-sided acrylic sanding pads referenced earlier. Wet sanding with MicroMesh™ is sometimes done, but if I use the acrylic finishing pads I always wet sand with them. CA is a form of plastic.

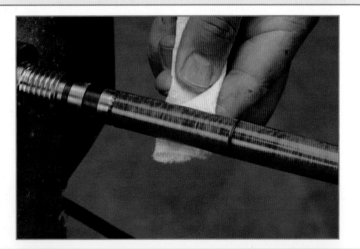

On the left half, CA glue alone will be used. CA is placed on the paper towel applicator and then applied to the spinning blank. Other applicators work well also.

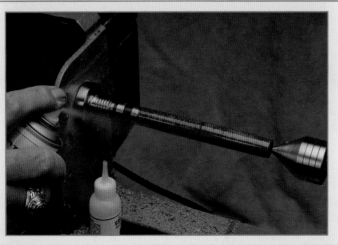

A light spray of accelerator from an aerosol can is applied after each coat of CA. I put on CA glue in thin layers and often use five or six layers, applying accelerator between each one. The accelerator is a mild one and only one short blast is used.

Lengthwise sanding with 400 grit paper is being done prior to wet sanding with the acrylic sanding pads.

Wet sanding is done with the acrylic sanding pads that I have mentioned several times. Buffing was done using NOVUS™ Plastic Polish #3 and #2.

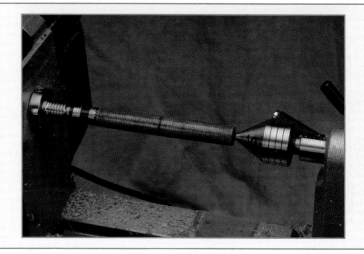

The spindle finished with CA glue and boiled linseed oil on the right half and CA glue alone on the left half. Both are easy and produce my favorite finish.

CA glue gets a bad rap as being a difficult finish to apply. I really don't understand why some have so much trouble using CA glue as a finish. If hearing that it is a difficult finish has some defeated before trying, they try it expecting to fail and they meet those expectations. CA glue with or without boiled linseed oil is an easy and fast finish to apply. I routinely apply six or more coats, sand, buff, and have the finish complete in ten minutes or so. Give it a try!

Some turners use Delrin™ rods and make a special bushing for finishing. CA glue will not stick to Delrin. Special bushings for use with CA glue for finishing are available and are made from Delrin. My suggestion would be to wax standard bushings with a paste wax and the glue will not stick to them. Thin CA glue will wick between the blank and the bushing and possibly glue the bushing to the mandrel. Be careful if using thin. Soak bushings stuck to a mandrel with CA glue in acetone. Acetone is the release agent for CA glue.

THE CHALLENGE PEN

The challenge pen, as I call it, is a design I was challenged to make. The challenge came from a friend who had made the pen, sent me a picture of it, and challenged me to make one. The only information I had was the picture. Hence the name "challenge pen." I was challenged to make one and making it *was* a challenge. But this design has led me to make other pens using this same design. Later a project will take this same design and use a unique material for the upper section.

The two barrels are made using three sections of wood. I normally use one wood for the center section and another wood for the other two sections. Let's get started and make this pen.

A previously made pen and the 3 blank sections I will use for project #7 are shown together. The center blank is cocobolo and the two end section blanks are African blackwood. The lengths of the blanks I will use for this project are 1.3", 3.1", and .5" These lengths may be changed to suit personal tastes. They are not written in stone. I often make the lower blank 1.5" long. The upper end of the center blank and the lower end of the upper blank are cut to 15°.

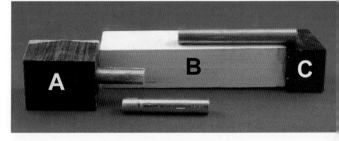

Section A is the blank for the nib end. Section B and Section C will be glued onto the tube to form the upper barrel. Other parts are shown relative to their position in the finished pen. The tube for the upper barrel is a normal length tube.

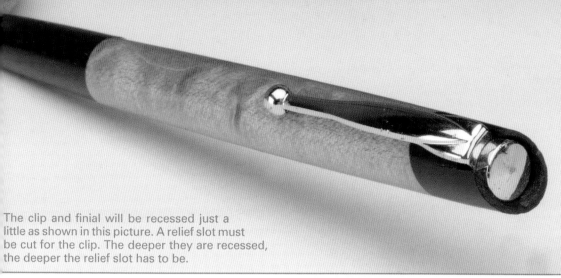

The clip and finial will be recessed just a little as shown in this picture. A relief slot must be cut for the clip. The deeper they are recessed, the deeper the relief slot has to be.

This picture shows my favorite recessed position for the clip and finial. The deeper they are recessed the longer the relief will need to be for the clip. My next favorite depth is where the clip clears with no relief cut needed. The finial is a little taller on the short side of the blank's bevel cut.

The square ends of these three blank sections need to be milled with a pen mill as normally done. The angled ends that will mate with each other need to be flat. Sanding them lightly with sandpaper on a flat surface will insure the fit will be tight with no gaps. I place sandpaper on my table saw table and lightly sand the two angled surfaces.

In my shop I use a power miter saw with an 80 tooth thin kerf blade to cut these blanks. They can be cut on a band saw but more sanding will be needed for the surfaces that mate together. A table saw can also be used but I suggest the use of a sled when cutting pen blanks on a table saw. Above all: SAFETY FIRST!

The section that will house the clip and finial will be made first. I will drill first and cut the blank to length later. You will see why I do it this way. I am holding the blank with a scroll chuck and pin jaws. A 7mm hole is being bored for the 7mm brass tube.

Without changing the blank's position in the chuck, I will now chase the 7mm hole with a 9/32" bit. This is the size needed for the clip and finial to fit inside. I suggest measuring the parts from the pen kit used and pick the appropriate drill bit size. The depth of the larger hole will be adjusted next for fit. For now, make the hole's depth about 3/4" deep.

The 15° cut has been made removing as little material as possible. Next, the clip and finial will be positioned. Actually, the finial will be fitted first.

The finial has been dropped into the hole. The deeper the hole, the further in the finial will fall. It can be left deeper and a relief for the clip will need to be cut. Remove a little more wood and the clip will clear the blank's edge and no relief will be needed. Choose the look that you like and go with it.

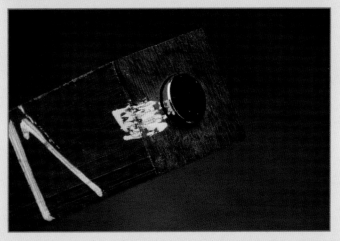

I have cut off a little more of the blank's end so the finial is exposed on the lower side of the bevel and just about flush with the high side of the bevel. The white marking next to the finial shows where the relief cut will be needed.

The section of blank is cut to the size I want. I decided to have the finial flush with the lower side of the bevel and a relief cut will be needed. When the tube is glued into place the tube's top needs to stop at the bottom of the larger hole. If you allow it to go further, the final will not position itself where planned.

The position of the brass tube is shown. It must be positioned at the bottom of the larger hole for the finial's placement to be where planned. If glued lower into the upper barrel then the finial will not press into the tube enough to hold the clip. The angled sides between the larger and smaller hole are formed by the drill bit if a standard bit is used.

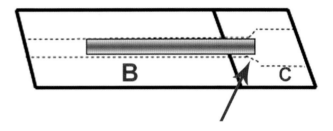

The cocobolo section with the 15° slice to match the clip end blank is mounted in a scroll chuck and a 7mm hole is being drilled. I am drilling from the square end to eliminate drill bit drifting on the 15° cut end.

Use a brass tube over the pilot shaft of a pen mill and square the non angled end of the cocobolo section. The two upper barrel sections are ready to be glued to the brass tube. Follow the positioning directions from above to get the brass tube in the correct position.

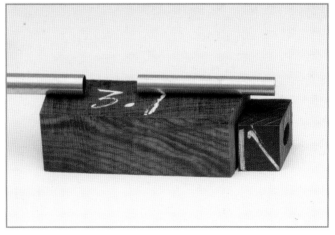

Here is where a very nice saw blade comes in handy. Smooth and accurate cuts will help ensure the angled surfaces mate together nice and tight. Sand the surfaces if necessary to get a good and tight joint.

The other section of blackwood needs to be drilled with a 7mm bit. The tube is glued into the blank. The wood blank is shorter than the tube, so about an inch of tube will be exposed. Not to worry, this is the way it should be. Square the end and mount the blank on the mandrel.

The lower section can be rough turned and shaped just a little. Do not complete it yet. All three pieces will be placed on the mandrel and turned as a single piece so the final shape can be seen as it develops.

The end of the lower blank, where the brass tube is exposed, needs to be squared using a parting tool. The pen mill cannot be used here. Flat and square will help ensure a nice joint where it meets the other part of the pen.

The two part glued blank is ready to mount on the mandrel. Use two or three Slimline bushings. The larger hole in the clip end will slide right over one of the Slimline bushings and press against the brass tube. This is another reason the brass tube placement is important.

Slide a 7mm tube into the cocobolo blank until it hits the tube glued into the other end. Place a Slimline bushing on and tighten the brass nut.

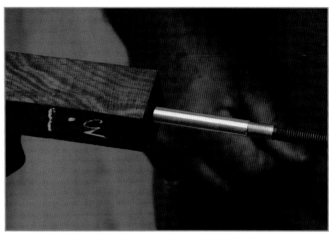

The end of the cocobolo blank can also be squared using a parting tool or a square carbide tool as I am doing here. Once the end is squared, remove the brass nut, bushing and extra tube.

Place the blackwood nib end blank that has been rounded (it has a section of tube exposed) onto the mandrel with the exposed tube inside the cocobolo blank. The pen will be turned as one unit. Check the fit of the two surfaces and adjust if needed.

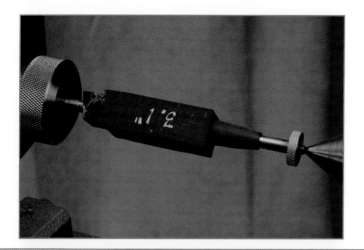

Replace the bushing and brass nut and tighten the nut and tail stock. The pen is ready to turn. Notice I use longer Slimline bushing. I like the extra length and the room they give on the ends of the blank. The shorter busing used in twos or threes also work.

The pen sections are being turned and shaped as a single unit. Turning this way allows the shape of the pen to be seen with all of the parts together. Continue shaping and turning until the desired shape and diameters are achieved. Several shapes are possible.

Turning is complete and the pen is ready to be sanded and the finish applied.

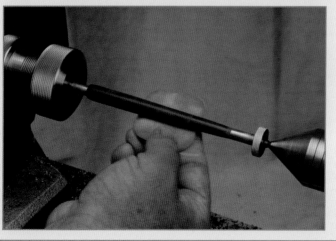

Sanding has been done to 600 grit and WATCO™ Danish Oil has been applied to darken the wood and accent the grain. Sanding is now being done with MicroMesh™ pads.

The pen is now ready for a finish to be applied. No finish is shown in this picture. Only a small amount of buffing has been done with a micro fiber cloth.

It is now time to cut the relief slot for the clip, if needed. I use a Dremel™ tool with a round burr to start the cutting. A file will be used later to square the corners. Take care not to break the unsupported wood above the tube. The thinner this part was turned, the more fragile it will be.

Rough cut the slot with a Dremel™ tool, paying attention to both the width and depth of the relief slot. Cut a little, test fit the clip, and continue until the clip fits the slot and clears the blank.

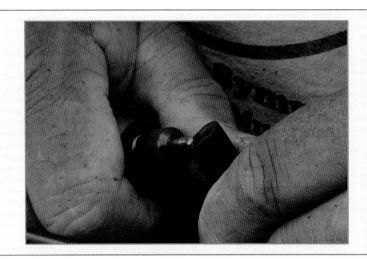

Once the notch has been roughed out with the Dremel™ tool, a microfile is used to finalize the shape and clean up the notch.

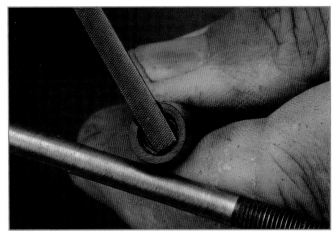

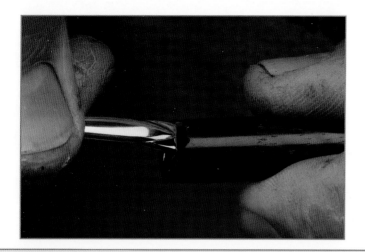

While test fitting the clip, I see I need to file the opening a little wider. Keep test fitting and filing until you have a snug fit.

Press in the finial and clip assembly, the nib, and the transmission as normal. The length from transmission end to nib end is still 3.95". Here is a view of the pen from the top.

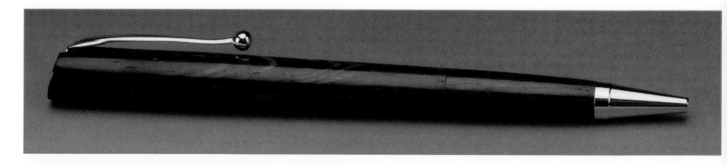

Another view of the completed pen taken from the side. This view gives a better look at the unique features of the pen.

CHALLENGE PEN VARIATION

Arrow Shaft Pen

The next pen will be a variation of the challenge pen. I will be replacing the upper two blank sections with a single section of hunting arrow shaft. I use aluminum arrows but arrows made from other materials should work. Some arrow shaft inner diameters are real close to the outer diameter of 7mm brass tubes, and a section of 7mm brass tube can be glued into the section of arrow shaft just like gluing a brass tube in a pen blank. Personally, I prefer a larger arrow shaft. The one I like is too large for gluing in a brass tube. I turn a wooden sleeve with a bead on one end to hold the clip and finial. The brass tube is inside the sleeve. Here is how it is done.

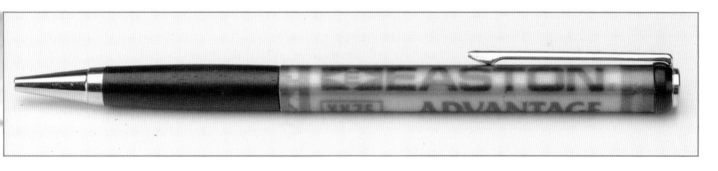

This is the pen to be made in project #8. The design is basically the challenge pen with the cocobolo-blackwood upper section replaced with an arrow shaft section. The arrow shaft section I use is **3.5"** long.

I use two different arrow sizes for the arrow shaft pen. The larger diameter arrow shaft requires a shim to be made to insert inside the arrow shaft section. The other is smaller but has an inside diameter just a little larger than the 7mm tube's outer diameter. For this one I use a section of 5/16" OD (outer diameter) tube glued inside the arrow shaft and into the 7mm tube will be glued inside this tube. The 5/16" tube could be replaced with a wooden shim as will be done for the pen in this project.

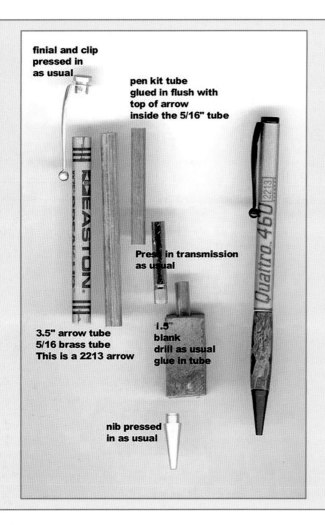

finial and clip
pressed in
as usual

pen kit tube
glued in flush with
top of arrow
inside the 5/16" tube

Press in transmission
as usual

3.5" arrow tube
5/16 brass tube
This is a 2213 arrow

1.5"
blank
drill as usual
glue in tube

nib pressed
in as usual

The parts for an arrow shaft pen using the smaller arrow shaft mentioned above. The arrow is a #2213. Notice the parts are basically the parts for the challenge pen with the upper two part barrel replaced with the section of arrow shaft.

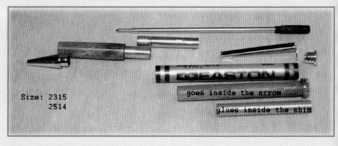

Size: 2315
2514

goes inside the arrow

glues inside the shim

The parts for the arrow pen made with the larger shaft are shown in relation to their placement in the completed pen. This arrow used here is either a #2315 or #2414.

The pen from a previous picture is shown with the parts to be used to make the pen in project 8. They are laid out in relation to how they will fit together. Notice the wooden shim has a bead on the end to give the clip and finial a place to seat. It also adds a nice feature to the pen. The shim is made from the same wood as the lower section.

To make the shim for the arrow shaft section, I have cut a piece of blackwood the same length as the arrow shaft section. One of the kit tubes is glued with an end flush with one end of the blank. This end will be the clip/finial end and will have the bead turned on the end. There will be a lot of turning and test fitting the arrow. The wood blank could be held between bushings with the brass nut but taking off the blank to test fit the arrow gets a little cumbersome. So, I will be using either the expanding closed end mandrel or the pin chuck to hold the blank so test fitting the arrow shaft will be much easier and quicker

Here is the expanding mandrel that can be used to hold the blank. These expanding mandrels are available from Arizona Silhouette at www.arizonasilhouette.com

The expanding mandrel is inserted into the blank from the end where the tube is flush with the end of the blank. A wrench is used to turn the nut, expanding the mandrel inside the tube to hold the blank securely.

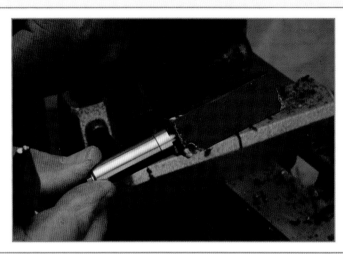

A pin chuck is another tool that can be used to hold the blank. With the pin chuck, the diameter of the chuck's shaft must be very close to the ID (inner diameter) of the pen tube.

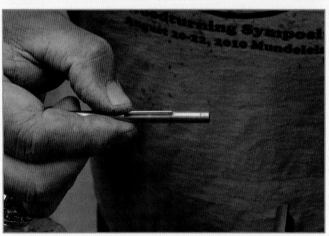

The pin chuck's shaft with the pin in its slot is inserted into the brass tube and the tube rotated and the pin locks the blank in place. Rotating the blank in the opposite direction will unlock the blank from the chuck's shaft.

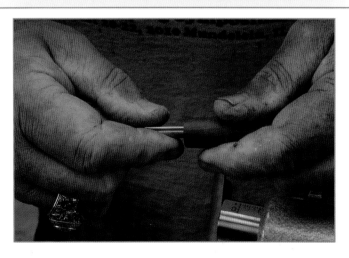

The wood shim has been turned with a bead on the clip end of the shim. The bead is turned down to .435". The shim has been reduced to .333", which slides inside the arrow shaft.

It is important for the pen clip to clear the bead when placed over the end of the shim. Test fitting or measuring will both work. When the shim is completed, the bead needs to be sanded and finished prior to gluing the shim in the arrow shaft.

The fit is good, so the bead end of the shim can be sanded and a finish applied.

The bottom barrel is turned exactly like the bottom barrel on the challenge pen. Square the end where the brass tube is exposed with a parting tool or the tip of a skew or a square cutter carbide tool. Also, the interface where the wood of the lower barrel meets the arrow shaft should be close to the diameter of the arrow. Just a little larger looks okay, but smaller is not good. The outer diameter of the arrow shaft is .367". It is wise to measure your arrow shaft for yourself rather than relying on this dimension.

The lower barrel is now turned to the correct size. Sand and apply a finish and the pen will be ready to assemble.

Test fit the lower barrel section into the arrow shaft assembly to make sure the parts all fit. The pen is now ready to be assembled. Assembly is straightforward. Press the nib into the end of the lower wooden barrel. Press the transmission into the other end of the lower barrel. Remember the length from nib tip to transmission tip is 3.95". Press the clip and finial into the arrow shaft end with the bead.

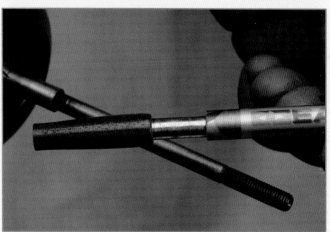

The completed pen is shown, although I just noticed the arrow shaft section is not the same one as in the project pictures. I just used a different arrow shaft section and didn't catch it in time to change.

THE ONE PIECE SLIMLINE

I first saw the one piece Slimline several years ago in one of Dick Sing's books. I have just recently started making them and have discovered a couple of improvements. I talked with Dick about these improvements a while ago and one of them he had also discovered. I have also incorporated the one piece Slimline and the challenge pen to make a challenge pen blank glued into one blank. This makes it into a one piece Slimline style. I have also played with several shapes for the barrel. I hope those of you who make this pen enjoy it as much as I have. It is a fun pen to make and use.

Once the mechanics of the one piece Slimline are understood, it is a simple and clever design. Twisting is accomplished by holding the nib and twisting the one piece body. I think both of the improvements I have found make twisting easier, along with pulling the pen apart to change the refill.

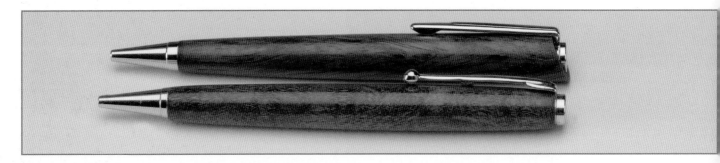

Two one piece Slimlines are shown in this picture. Notice the top pen has the challenge pen feature on the clip end. This is done exactly the same way as in the challenge pen. Project #9 will be making the bottom version and the top version will be left as a challenge for those reading this book.

A one piece Slimline is shown with the barrel removed from the nib-tube-transmission assembly.

copyright Don Ward Red River Pens

This picture shows the parts of the pen positioned relative to their position in the completed pen. The nib-tube-transmission assembly has been assembled. The improvements are shown also.

Improvement #1: In the previous picture notice the short tube on the right just above the blank. This is an 8mm tube from a perfume pen or bracelet helper kit. Its length is about 3/4" and will be glued into the nib end of the pen. The 7mm tube into which the nib is pressed will slip through the 8mm tube. This short 8mm tube will serve two purposes. One is to add some strength to the end of the pen where the wood veneer is very thin. The other is to allow the nib-tube-transmission assembly to more freely twist without binding on the wood if the 8mm tube was not used. Be sure all burrs are removed from the ends of the 8mm tube section. Burrs will cause binding.

Improvement #2: The second kit tube which is the one to the left in the previous picture will only be partially inserted and glued into the clip end of the barrel. It will be inserted just enough to engage the transmission's end. The excess will be cut off. This will allow the pen to more easily be taken apart for refill replacement.

The blank for this pen is 4.25" long and squared on each end with a pen mill. A 7mm tube is used on the pen mill shaft as we have done previously. The blank for this pen has been turned to a diameter of 3/4". The wood is bloodwood.

The hardest part of this pen proved to be drilling a hole through the center of a blank that is longer than the drill bit. Read on to learn how this hole can be drilled.

Drilling the hole can be accomplished by using a long bit. Six inch aircraft bits are available. Some pen kit suppliers may carry them or they are available from industrial supply websites like McMaster-Carr, Enco, Grainger Supply or others. They may be available locally in some larger cities. Several of the pen kit suppliers carry Colt™ bits and they make a 7mm bit that is longer than normal.

To accomplish drilling this hole with a bit shorter than the blank, I use the 3/4" collet in my collet chuck to hold the previously rounded blank. I have excellent luck drilling the hole half way from one end then switching ends and drilling the other half from the other end. Having a consistent diameter also helps. I drill the clip end first, then swap ends and drill the nib end second. Drilling the nib end last allows me to drill the larger hole for the 8mm tube section without moving the blanks, ensuring the 8mm hole is concentric with the 7mm hole.

Replace the 7mm bit with a Letter O bit to counter drill an 8mm hole, enlarging the 7mm hole. The 8mm hole should be the same length as the section of 8mm tube being used.

Glue in the short section of 8mm brass tube.

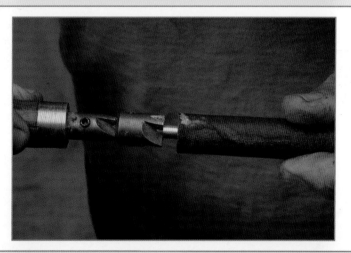

A pen mill with a 7mm tube over the pilot shaft is used to square the end of the blank after the 8mm tube section is glued in place. 8mm pen mill pilot shafts are available to be purchased.

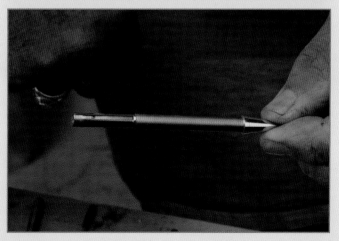

Press the nib into one end of one of the kit's tubes and press the transmission into the other end. Remember: **3.95"**.

Slide the nib-tube-transmission assembly into the blank through the 8mm tube glued in previously.

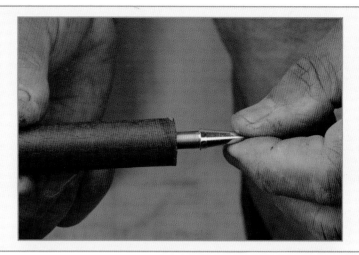

Holding the nib assembly firmly in place, slide the other kit tube into the other end of the blank. Push the tube onto the transmission just enough to grab the transmission and hold it firmly enough for the transmission to twist. The tube is 2.1" long and I used 1.3" of the tube inside the blank. The rest will be cut off and removed. Glue the shortened tube in place. Once the shorter tube section is glued into place, square the end with the pen mill as before.

A section of brass tube needs to be inserted through the 8mm tube until it hits the tube glued into the clip end. Cut off the excess exposed part of the tube. This tube is needed while the blank is being turned. Do not glue this tube in place. It will be removed and not used in the final version of the pen.

Place the blank from the previous picture on the mandrel with bushings and tighten the brass nut. The blank is ready to be turned into a pen barrel.

Important note: I have the nib end towards the headstock. Please remember where you place the nib end and do not forget and turn the pen backwards. It will not work that way! The nib end and clip end cannot be switched. The end with the 8mm short tube has to be the nib end. Accidentally switching them is easy. It is easy to forget which end is the nib end and which end is the clip end. Don't ask me how I know that! I have switched ends more than once.

The barrel is rounded down to its final shape. Sanding and applying a finish is the next step.

The barrel is complete for this single piece pen and the finish has been applied. Press the clip and finial in place and slide the nib-tube-transmission in place and the pen is ready to use.

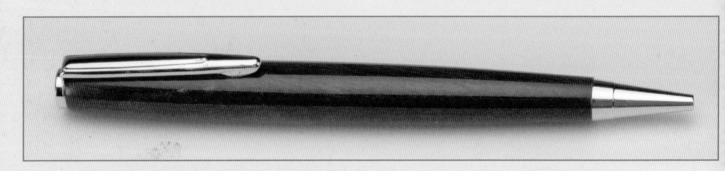

The completed pen is ready to use. The pen has a unique look and lots of design possibilities. What a fun project!

Here are a few more hints I have found handy.

I place dots on the side of my micro-mesh pads to help me get them in order after they have been mixed up, which seems to happen often. One dot on the 1500 pad, two dots on the 1800, three dots on the 2400 and so on.

Miniature microfiles and dental picks come in handy. These sets were purchased from Harbor Freight Tools.

BATTER UP!
A BASEBALL BAT SLIMLINE

For the last project of this book I have chosen to have a little fun and use the parts from a Slimline kit to make a pen in the shape of a baseball bat. Getting the correct proportions for the bat proved to be the most difficult for me. I turned several small bats from blanks held between centers. Finally, I found the shape and proportions that looked pleasing to me. The wood for this pen is a piece of figured mesquite.

The pen can be made in several ways. The nib can be on the handle end or the business end of the bat. The clip can be used or not used. I have chosen to make the baseball bat pen with the nib on the handle end with no clip. This means the fat end will not have a hole drilled all the way through the blank. This type of hole is called a blind hole. How does one hold a pen blank on a mandrel if the hole does not go all the way through? Hmmm!

One of my baseball bat pens using Slimline parts is shown with the blank cut for this final project. The handle end uses one of the Slimline tubes, so it was cut to the proper length. The other part of the blank was used for the business end of the bat-pen. A hole was drilled deep enough for the other tube to be glued in place. The final length of the fat end of the bat is 3.25". These lengths can be adjusted as desired.

The blank for the handle end has been drilled, the tube is glued in place and the ends have been squared with the pen mill. The blank is on the mandrel awaiting its turning.

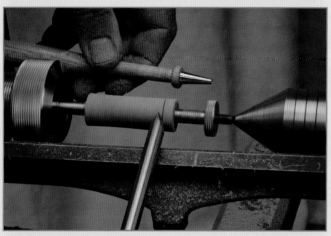

The handle end is round and the handle knob is being marked. The knob width is about 1/8" but I marked it a little longer and worked it to final width. The diameter of the knob end is about .55".

The handle is being shaped. Stop before final diameter is reached so the other blank can be added and the bat turned as a unit. This is much the same as we did with the challenge pen.

The other blank section has been drilled and the tube glued in place. The end has been squared. The handle has been turned around and the other blank is placed on the mandrel. The tailstock provides enough pressure to hold the blanks tight enough to turn the bat as a single unit.

The bat is taking shape. Continue to turn the bat.

A detail gouge with a fingernail grind is used to add the final shapes and detail to the bat-shaped pen. The bat shape is almost done.

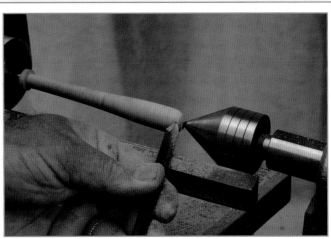

Shaping the handle knob with the detail gouge.

The bat is ready for sanding and applying a finish. This is done now on the handle part and the fat end where the tailstock is will be worked on next. Remove the fat end and place the bushing back on the mandrel. Screw on the brass nut and tighten. Sand and apply the finish to the handle section.

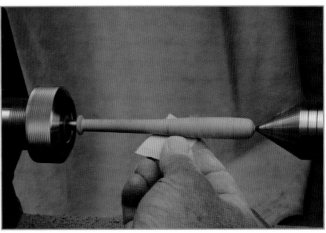

Remove the mandrel and replace it with the pin chuck used earlier. I will hold the fat end of the bat with the pin chuck to shape the end where the live center was holding the blank. It will be sanded and the finish applied. The rest of the bat has had the finish applied already.

An alternative to using a pin chuck, or the 7mm expanding mandrel for closed end pens, to hold the blank, is to use blue tape and tape the blank to the mandrel. The tape will hold the blank secure enough for the end to be completed.

Remember the pin chuck or the expanding mandrel for closed end pens? Here is a good use for one of them. Blue tape or masking tape also works.

The live center mark is being removed and the fat end of the bat is taking shape.

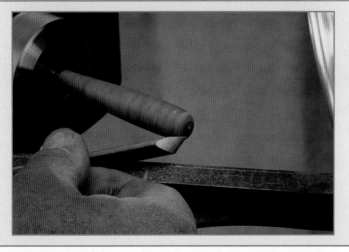

The end is almost completed. Just a little more work is needed. Sand and apply the finish.

Once again, assembly is standard. The only difference, unless the fat end of the bat is to have a clip and finial, the clip and finial will not be used. Press the nib and transmission in place, add the refill and put the fat end of the bat over the transmission and push into place.

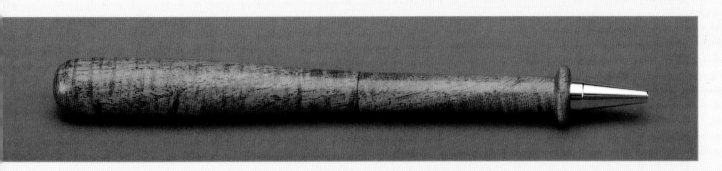

The completed pen is shown, although I just noticed the arrow shaft section is not the same one as in the project pictures. I just used a different arrow shaft section and didn't catch it in time to change.

THE COMPLETED
PROJECTS

Here are pictures of the projects presented in this book.

The pen from Project #1 is a Slimline made from maple burl. The pen is made according to the manufacturer's instructions.

The pen from Project #2 made from bocote with African blackwood accent band.

The pen from Project #3 made from bubinga. The accent band is a slice of credit card.

The pen and pencil set from Project #4 made from walnut. The accent rings are slices of guitar pick guard.

Project #5 uses a rifle cartridge for the lower barrel and a real bullet for the nib.
The upper barrel is a piece of camouflage pattern acrylic.

Project #7 is my challenge pen made using cocobolo and African blackwood.

Project #8 is basically the challenge pen with the upper barrel replaced with a section of arrow shaft.

Project #9 is the one piece Slimline made using bloodwood.

Project 10 is a pen shaped like a baseball bat. The wood is figured mesquite.

GALLERY
PENS

Five pens made in the Don Line style. The center pen is antler.

Another set of Don Line pens. The bottom pen has a center band from a designer or Euro pen I found in a box of parts. The second pen up from the bottom is made with inlaid stars. The stars and the "star" holes along with the thin slices were cut using a laser.

A collection of one piece Slimline pens.

Another set of Don Line pens using snake skin blanks for the top.
The blanks have a wooden slice from the left over blank used on the pen's bottom.

Four challenge pens. The top pen has the upper barrel made with leather disks.

A trio of challenge pens with arrow shaft sections are shown.

The top pen has a closed end on the cap and the clip has been recessed into the cap. The center pen sports a twist cut on a small mill and the bottom pen has a nib, center band, and finial made from African blackwood.

Several pens made using rifle and pistol cartridges.

The top three pens are made using rattlesnake skin cast under polyester resin. The blanks were made by the author. The bottom two pens are made using pheasant feathers cast under polyester resin. The blanks were made by John Underhill and are available from www.exoticblanks.com.

Four pens made using blanks cast with polyester resin. The computer blank was purchased from www.arizonasilhouette.com. The other blanks used were cast by the author. The bottom pen has stamp images printed on a peel and stick mailing label. The third blank down from the top is made using shredded money purchased from the US Bureau of Engraving and the top pen is coffee beans cast in white resin.

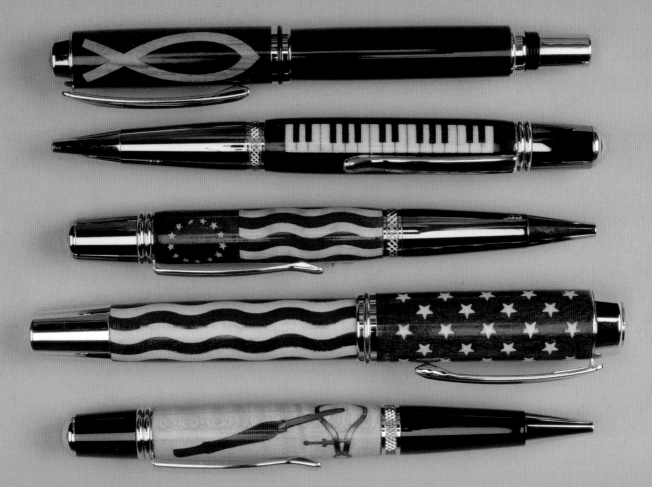

Pens made using laser cut inlay blanks from www.kallenshaanwoods.com.

These pens are made from blanks made using polymer clay. The floral design is similar to a glasswork technique known as millefiori. I obtained the blanks from the very talented and accomplished award winning polymer clay artist Toni Ransfield of New Jersey. More of her work can be seen at www.exclusivedesignz.com/aboutus/ and her blanks are available from www.exoticblanks.com.